April 1999

Dear Louise,

  May this small book delight your senses and contribute to the joy of being a garde

Foxgloves
and
Hedgehog Days

ILLUSTRATIONS BY
CATHERINE ROSE CROWTHER

A Frances Tenenbaum Book
HOUGHTON MIFFLIN COMPANY
BOSTON · NEW YORK
1997

DANIEL BLAJAN

Foxgloves and Hedgehog Days

SECRETS
IN A
COUNTRY
GARDEN

For information about permission to reproduce
selections from this book, write to
Permissions, Houghton Mifflin Company,
215 Park Avenue South, New York,
New York 10003.

For information about this and other
Houghton Mifflin trade and reference books
and multimedia products, visit The Bookstore
at Houghton Mifflin on the World Wide Web
at http://www.hmco.com/trade/.

Library of Congress Cataloging-in-Publication Data
Blajan, Daniel
Foxgloves and hedgehog days : secrets in a
country garden / Daniel Blajan
p.   cm.
"A Frances Tenenbaum Book"
ISBN 0-395-85729-5
1. Gardening. 2. Country life. 3. Gardening —
Netherlands. 4. Country life — Netherlands.
5. Blajan, Daniel. I. Title.
SB455.B538   1997   96-43524
949.2'4 — DC21   CIP

Printed in the United States of America

Book design by Robert Overholtzer

QUM 10 9 8 7 6 5 4 3 2 1

*To me every hour of the light and the dark
is a miracle,
Every cubic inch of space is a miracle.*

— WALT WHITMAN, "Miracles"

Contents

Foxgloves
and
Hedgehog Days

A Word of Warning

IS YOUR HOME a shining example of domestic discipline? Does the slightest clutter on your desk put you in a state of monumental gloom? Is your garden always the quintessence of Apollonian perfection? Yes? Then this book is not meant for you, and please be so kind as to put it back where you found it. It will not guide you on your wanderings toward further fulfillment, and it will certainly not enlighten any aspect within your range of interests. You will learn nothing from it. On the contrary, its macaronic undertone is likely to disgust you, and consequently it does not deserve a place on your neatly arranged bookshelves, not even on the very bottom one. By the way, I envy you, for your life is unlikely to be a perpetual struggle against overflowing cupboards and ever-lengthening lists of Things To Do that are somehow never done.

I won't keep you any longer, for although you're more than welcome to stay, I've a sneaking suspicion that you're dying to continue along your own straight and well-defined paths. So in case we don't meet again, may God bless you — and have a very nice life.

If, however, you keep your postage stamps in a tea caddy, if the only roses in your garden are of the rambling variety and thrive in chaotic harmony, and if your shedding cat is allowed to claim your best chair at all hours — if, in short, you are blessed with a proclivity for inspired imbroglio — well, then these writings might just be your cup of tea. You might find the pages laced with fleeting moments of magic. You might delight in the small miracles that I intend to reveal to you, such as the voice of pine cones and the secret of weeping irises. You might even shed a tear occasionally, for in our dealings with Mother Nature we can hardly ignore one of her main characteristics: transience. And transience, you will agree, rarely disposes the mind to gaiety.

A word of warning, however. This is not a how-to book. If you look for any kind of practical guidance in your daily doings, alas, you will find none. Neither will you find scientific solutions to mysteries or explanations for miracles, for once explained, miracles cease to exist, and I much prefer to make miracles part of my daily life

— and, I hope, yours as well. After all, isn't life itself the ultimate miracle?

Therefore I invite you to stroll along my border, which is more like a jungle of weeds, and discover its secrets. To take a brisk walk through the surrounding fields and pine woods. To sit in my garden after the last long shadows have dissolved into darkness and listen to the sounds of the night. To . . .

No, I shall not disclose anything else yet. Just stay with me, and I am certain that you will enjoy these exciting explorations as much as I do, and that they will open your eyes and your ears, so that all of a sudden you will begin to discover and recognize your own private miracles all around you. And should this be the case, well, then this book will turn out to be a how-to book after all, in a sort of spiritual way.

By the way, I must now confess that this is not really the first chapter. Rather, it is a foreword. However, since I discovered that many people skip forewords, I opted against calling it one. Can you forgive me?

Earwigs

OR THE RECORD it must now be noted that I
have not always been a country dweller. In fact,
most of my life has evolved within the periphery of
metropolitan bustle. But the rural ways of living were
never entirely strange to me. As a boy I spent many a
school vacation with my grandmother or one of my
aunts in the country, and some cherished childhood
memories have stayed with me until this very day: the
feel of wet grass under my bare feet, the sound of coffee
bubbling through the old-fashioned percolator, the
smell of homemade sausages sizzling in the pan, the
taste of freshly baked soda bread at teatime, and the
thrilling horror of regiments of earwigs dropping from
huge bunches of garden-fresh dahlias and parading over

the kitchen table. Not that I cherished the earwigs at the time. On the contrary, they never failed to give me the creeps, as I sincerely believed them to have designs on ears, mine in particular — why else should they be called earwigs? Of course as I grew older, I learned that this was nothing but an old wives' tale, and after I spent years of a somewhat neurotic existence in my sixth-floor city apartment, the very thought of earwigs was enough to evoke memories of rural bliss. They became a symbol of the sweet earth. But not once in those fifteen years did I catch a single live earwig in the act of lurking in shop-bought flowers or between pleats of curtains and stacked linens. There were flies, of course, and the occasional cockroach, although owing to our rather sterile living conditions, or possibly the evil traffic fumes, these did not put in frequent appearances, and they failed to become a symbol of anything.

Having said that, I still recall with unusual clarity the one occasion on which a very single and lonely earwig honored me with a visit. It crawled out of a delightfully entangled bouquet of roses presented to me by a friend, "out of her own garden." It marched over the glass-topped coffee table and tried in vain to hide under the monstrous Baccarat ashtray. I caught it in a paper napkin, for nothing will induce me to touch an earwig with my bare hands, and I wondered what to do with it. Toss it out the window? Somehow opening a sixth-floor window while an unexpected summer storm raged over the city seemed impractical, and anyway, the earwig almost certainly would not survive traffic conditions down below. So I flushed it, eyes closed (for I'm a coward), and I felt very sorry for it.

But its ghost lingered on, and in the weeks that followed I remembered at intervals how pathetic it had looked on the glass-topped, chromium-framed table. I could not help thinking that it would have been much happier with solid oak under its panicky little feet. Like the massive table in my aunt's home in the country, I thought with a twinge of nostalgia. And all of a sudden it seemed an excellent idea to do away with my contemporary chromium and nickel and steel. I had been lounging too long on Charles Eames and Mies Van Der Rohe, and the strict regime of rigid lines and corners sharp as knives had begun to cut into my soul. It was time to replace it with something more . . . more what? I had absolutely no idea. My imagination had almost become like my furniture: inflexible, unyielding, transparent.

Then one of my aunts died and I inherited a few pieces of her furniture. Much as I regretted her demise, it gave me a welcome excuse to get rid of some of my twentieth-century contraptions. Out went two steel-framed easy chairs. And, of course, the coffee table. A year later another dear aunt gave up her house in the country and moved into a smaller home. She bestowed on me an enormous and somewhat rustic antique farm table that would easily withstand a dancing competition on its top, and eight mismatched yet delightfully vintage chairs that evoked visions of candlelight and crinolines and rustling taffeta. They also brought back memories of long summer vacations and warm apple pies in my aunt's kitchen and mysterious gun lockers in my uncle's study and a procession of cats jumping in and out through the kitchen window the livelong day.

I was as pleased as Punch with these additions, and gradually I began to develop a taste for "Country," a word that had not yet acquired its present fashionable flavor and was certainly never spelled with a capital *C*. I frequented flea markets and auction houses and purchased the occasional piece to match my new possessions, mostly in an attempt to revive the spirit of my aunt's old country home. Sane people indulge in the future, but I indulged in the past. I wanted the soft glow of old, polished wood, the muted colors of faded, slightly threadbare carpets, bowls brimming with potpourri. Not because these latter were in vogue; they weren't at the time. "Dead flowers? You must be out of your mind!" was a frequent comment from my friends. But merely because they echoed years of sheltered happiness. There was nothing exotic about it; the potpourri of my youth was, after all, as much a household item as kitchen cleanser and dishwashing liquid.

I have to admit, in retrospect, that my efforts were spectacularly unsuccessful. If anything, the apartment now resembled a glorified junk shop rather than even the humblest of country houses. It was not until much later, when "Country" became a new trend and rapidly conquered urbanity, that I understood why: "Country" belongs in the country. Transferred to the city, it tends to be artificial, superfluous, and sometimes, I'm sorry to say, slightly ridiculous. What, for instance, could possibly be the use of an antique mud scraper in the hallway of a tenth-floor condo? Yet that is exactly what friends of mine have, mounted on the luxurious wall-to-wall carpet in their mirrored hall, the very last place where one would like to have mud scraped from shoes. And what on earth induced my neighbor to keep his cigars in a specially adapted and artificially weathered birdhouse, in which no bird with any self-respect would be caught dead?

But I'm straying, and we should really return as soon as possible to my own sixth-floor apartment and the earwig and my effort to create a country ambiance. At first I was satisfied, though admittedly my aunt's table was a little oversized, to say the least. And one could hardly fail to notice that the slightly tattered wing chairs positively clashed with the sleek radiators of the central heating. Instead they were screaming for a nice fireplace — an inglenook, preferably.

In the early eighties, when "Country" began to penetrate the city, I tasted my moment of triumph, as one by one my friends' apartments metamorphosed into chintzy paradises; I was generally but wrongly regarded as a trendsetter and admired for being so far ahead of fashion.

Yes, "Country" became big business. One day I found an entire floor of one of our big department stores smothered in frills and ruffles. Avalanches of dried flowers and oceans of countrified cotton prints poured from straw and wicker baskets that, strategically placed in the middle of the aisles, made it almost impossible to penetrate any further into this jungle of pastoralism — at least, not without knocking over some of the countless mass-produced wooden creatures that stared at me from tables and shelves and betrayed their country of origin with faintly oriental expressions. Beribboned geese especially were rampant in all sizes and ungoosely colors. (The ribboned goose appears to have gained so much popularity lately that I fear it is about to oust eagles and lions from heraldry.) The place oozed nostalgia, and one could not help being wafted, there and then, to the realms of *The Wind in the Willows*. It was all too delightful. It was also totally absurd.

Then my eye fell on the earwig. Not a live one. No, a giant cast-iron critter doubling as a boot-puller. I could not resist it, and I had paid for it before I knew what I was doing. But as it was being wrapped at the sales counter in soft tissue paper with a Provençal design, my friends' mud-scraper sprang to my mind, and my neighbor's ridiculous birdhouse–cigar box. Could it be that I was now on the verge of joining their ranks with a purchase that was to have no function at all? Unless, of course, I acquired a proper pair of boots with it.

At precisely that moment somewhere a spectral door opened and in stalked It, with a smug grin on Its ghostly face. "When you live in the country," It muttered, "you'll *need* boots. And probably more than just one pair." It chuckled a ghastly chuckle, rubbed Its transparent hands, and retired again, carefully closing the door behind It and leaving me in a state of well-calculated shock. At that very moment I realized I was about to make a decision that would inevitably result in nights of insomnia and days of splitting headaches and sinister red numbers on my bank statements. What was I about to let myself in for? But by the end of the week I had made up my mind: I was ready to say farewell to city life. Three months later I moved out of my apartment in The Hague and into a small cottage in an extremely rural area close to a tiny village near the Belgian border.

That was six years ago, and I have never regretted my rash decision. I would rather miss out on a live performance of Beethoven's *Emperor* than on nature's symphony of the morning birdsong and the wind in the trees. What would life be without fresh flowers, gathered from the garden or the wild almost daily? Or without our romantic, albeit slightly annoying, power outages, which justify reserving an entire shelf for boxes of candles in all shapes and sizes and colors?

And the earwigs? Well, for some obscure reason, this summer earwigs have been abundant, both outside and indoors. Just now, as I settled down to finish these words, one crawled out from between the keys of my word processor. It hardly disturbed me. I picked it up with a piece of tissue (I still refuse to touch them with my bare hands) and threw it out into the garden, where, I hope, it will soon find its way into a cozy dahlia and live happily ever after.

A Ballet in the Border

TREES STRETCHING their branches toward the azure sky, leaves whispering in the wind, flowers dancing in the air — well-worn phrases; we read these arabesque descriptions in books and magazines all the time. I too am often guilty of letting flowery phraseology freely flow from my pen when I indulge in describing our flora. It deserves it, though. After all, what could possibly be more flowery than our floral world, and I'm grateful for the existence of so many positive adjectives. Nevertheless, many an author has frequently and unintentionally suggested motion and sound, almost as if branches, leaves, and flowers were creatures of flesh and blood. We know better, of course. Trees don't wave their branches about like the arms of a frolicking octopus —

at least, not without a twenty-five-mile-an-hour wind. And without a breeze, leaves will refuse to utter a single whisper and flowers will remain perfectly motionless.

True, to a certain extent the very act of growing implies motion and sound, but however fast a seedling reaches up, it is still too slow for the human eye to perceive. And you will agree that the sound of a flower unfolding its petals is simply too silly even to contemplate. Or is it?

I know it is not. Over and over again I have marveled at the ability of plants, flowers, and seeds to produce sounds and motions that, however subtle, are audible and visible, if only we open our ears and eyes to them. I know beyond any doubt that some flowers *do* whisper and dance, preferably when there is no wind at all. Let me reveal this little miracle, for it is worth sharing.

In my kindergarten years I used to spend the summer holidays with my grandmother, who at the time lived in a small village in the heart of the Dutch tulip fields. How well I remember those happy sun- and fun-filled days of frog catching, tree climbing, and cat chasing (though more often than not the enormous and vicious tomcat chased me). The days seemed endless, but bedtime never failed to sneak up on me, even though I did all within my power to delay it. When my bag of tricks to postpone the dreaded moment for even one more minute was finally empty, a bedtime story would somewhat soften my annoyance at having to abandon my favorite pursuits. My grandmother had a very vivid imagination, and her nightly stories were always brimming with miracles and magic. As soon as humans had retired, tables and teapots allegedly came to life, chairs chattered, and yes, flowers chanted and danced. Of course I believed every word of her tales, but however hard I tried, I never succeeded in fooling pottery and furniture into believing that I was asleep and that therefore they were free to move about as they pleased. One night, however, I magnificently succeeded in cheating the flowers.

Behind the shed, well out of sight, I had my own little bit of land. This was my secret and sacred garden, untouched by the grownup world. Here lettuce and leek thrived in close harmony with daisy and dock, and in that particular year with a small jungle of oenothera, or evening primrose (though I must add for honesty's sake that at the time I was unfamiliar with this name).

Evening primrose. The very name vibrates with magic. It evokes visions of romping elves, of an Arthur Rackham illustration coming to life. And believe me, vibrate they do, these lovely flowers of the moon, and not only with magic, as I was about to discover.

One night, when my grandmother had treated me to a particularly vivid bedtime tale in which flowers merrily jumped about with elves and hobgoblins, I decided that it was high time to witness such a gay event with my own eyes. I crept out of bed and sneaked unobserved through the back door into the garden. It was not yet dark, but the sun had already set and it was one of those rare, serene nights when you feel you could almost catch the light and hold it in your hand like a shimmering violet treasure. A perfect night for the flowers to dance. I looked around the garden surreptitiously, but obviously all the flowers had already noticed my arrival, and they remained as stiff as pokers. I tiptoed to the shed and stealthily peeped around the wall. It was then that I beheld a great and breathtaking miracle: in the still of the night, the flowers of the evening primroses were coming to life. The pale yellow petals were unfolding one by one, flower after flower, like the wings of butterflies. They were unfolding at such speed that they caused the stems — yes, the whole plants — to tremble and quiver like a troupe of nervous ballerinas ready to jump on stage. My keen ears picked up their voices too: a soft, mysterious sighing, like whispers from elfin lips. Soon the night moths joined the party and began to feast on the nectar. In great numbers they flitted from flower to flower, adding even more grace to this floral ballet. I didn't move a finger; I just stood there, mesmerized by this magical *tableau vivant,* hardly daring to breathe lest I should break the magic of this performance, in which the flowers were the chorus girls dancing to the faint and rapid beat of trembling insects' wings.

I don't know how long I stood there, but I remember that all of a sudden the last glimmer of daylight faded away and it became too dark to see anything at all. In a state of utter bliss I slipped back into bed. That night, I knew, I had witnessed my very first miracle: the flowers had danced especially for me.

It was one of those rare moments that has remained silhouetted in my memory for all time, and when I moved to the country I decided that it could well be within my reach to recreate this episode. It needed some effort to achieve this, for initially my search for evening primroses yielded only some cultivated nursery varieties with huge yellow flowers and short stems. They were stunning enough, but absolutely refused to cooperate. Not in an entire season would they perform even a single simple *pas de deux*. They remained as limp and lifeless as handkerchiefs on a clothesline on a windless day. But one afternoon two years ago I chanced upon a nice clump of wild evening primroses, hiding in a corner of a deserted field at the outskirts of our village. I collected some of their seeds and sowed these in a sheltered corner behind the toolshed.

And now, after many years, the evening primroses once again dance for me, and for whoever cares to join me. In fact, this *Bal des Fleurs* has become one of the highlights of my summer season. On calm July evenings I put a chair out in this hidden spot. I sit down and wait.

I don't have to wait long: as soon as dusk sets in, the flowers come to life. They unfold with jerky spiraling movements, and their fragrance immediately attracts a multitude of night moths, thirsty after their long day of repose. Their wavering wings fill the air with agitated whispers. I absorb every detail of this phantasmagoria, feeling like royalty attending a command performance. My garden is the stage, the flowers and moths are the performers in this enchanted spectacle.

But nothing lasts, and after the last flower has unfurled in a final encore, the curtain of night falls over this miraculous ballet in the border. I retire for the evening, once again strengthened in my belief that he who does not believe in miracles leads an empty life indeed.

Miraculous Mushrooms

THOUGH I'M CONVINCED that I'm the world's worst gardener (and so, by the way, are many of my acquaintances — convinced, I mean), I love gardening. I really do. There is nothing like owning a patch of soil, one's very own tiny slice of our earth's surface. And "to grasp its scheme of things entire, and then remold it, nearer to the heart's desire" (to interpret Omar Khayyám's words freely) is one of life's great joys. However, while remolding my slice, a process which, by the way, goes forever on and on, I have developed an unfortunate penchant for uninvited guests. And believe me, in a rural and wooded area such as ours, there are many, and the struggle against weeds, seedlings, and mosses never ceases. But the true core of my problem is that I feel sorry for them, and it is with great reluctance that I pull them out. Sometimes I don't, and a couple of years ago I decided to declare a certain part of the garden "open house" for whatever has roots, leaves, or flowers, with the possible exception of some obnoxious grasses with tyrannical characteristics. This plot I have dubbed the Gnome Garden. Not because it is a home for some lurking plaster effigies. No. Brightly colored garden gnomes and I have never been on speaking terms. But because I feel that if the Little People really do exist — and who am I to contradict this? — they will be very happy in it. A theory which, by the way, I hope to exploit fully in a future chapter. Meanwhile, let us leave the gnomes in peace and return to the garden without further ado.

To me, this particular patch of neglect is a source of endless joy and numerous pleasant surprises. Not only to me, apparently. Under the hedge behind this sheltered plot lives a family of shrews. They emerge, usually during the evening, from their subterranean dwelling and start rummaging about in search of snails and slugs and insects. Worms too are on their menu, and the fact that these latter are sometimes twice their own size does not in the least deter them. It is fascinating to observe how they deal with a five-inch dinner (the shrews themselves are about two and a half inches long) with great determination, tugging and pulling at it until finally the last wormy fragment has vanished into their greedy stomachs.

The shrews also surprised me with one of the most delightful spectacles I have ever beheld in my garden. This is what I saw: a tiny but long snout carefully peeking out of its hole (I know its exact location) under the hedge and inspecting its surroundings. When all was presumed safe and clear, the rest of the body followed. But he, or she, was not alone, for another, much smaller snout followed, and another, and another, and . . . I couldn't believe my eyes, for there, in perfect formation, marched the entire family through the garden, a caravan of one adult in front and five children trailing behind it. Each individual firmly bit the back of its predecessor with the tip of its tapir-like little snout, and they looked altogether like an odd-shaped, furry millipede, zigzagging and meandering through the weeds.

Slowly, very slowly, I bent over to have a closer look at this phenomenon. Not slowly enough, however, for they noticed me immediately and flitted back into their nest, without once interrupting their formation. Later I learned that this is well-established and common shrew practice when parents take the children out for their first walk, yet I never witnessed such a performance again.

Not only shrews live in this plot of garden; during the day it is a favorite hangout for blackbirds, titmice, and a robin, who much prefer my wilderness to the disciplined regime of my neighbors' borders. From morning till night these birds can be seen, and heard, doing their useful bit of gardening, and they keep the place wonderfully free from pests.

Apart from the marvel of marching shrews, I have observed several miracles in the Gnome Garden. Minor ones, admittedly, but still my own private miracles. Let me give you an example.

One honey-colored morning this summer, I sat at the old cast-iron table enjoying my first cup of early morning tea. Meanwhile I was doing a visual inspection of all things growing, for it was during high season, when changes occur in rapid succession. You retire for the night with vague ideas about adding color to some dull corner of the garden, but in the morning you wake up to an altogether different decor, which immediately renders such plans obsolete. Suddenly all the rhododendrons are in flower and alive with bumblebees. Or you find that the green spikes of the foxgloves have turned overnight into candles of lilac and pink and white.

But that morning I spotted something unfamiliar and strange: a small globular object at the foot of the hedge behind the Gnome Garden. A stray Ping-Pong ball, perhaps? This seemed unlikely, for it had definitely not been there the previous day. An eggshell from the wood pigeons' nest? But no, the color and shape were all wrong. I conducted an immediate investigation and found it to be some kind of fungus. It was perfectly smooth and whitish and rubbery and unlike any other kind I had ever encountered. True to my policy of tolerance, I allowed the intruder to stay. I finished my tea and examined it a second time. Only now I discovered that it was not quite so smooth: there was a mysterious crack in its side, behind which something pinkish was lurking. How curious that I should have missed this obvious detail. I went in to get more tea, and when I returned I saw, to my utter amazement, that the aperture had widened and a little pink-and-bright-orange thing was timidly protruding through it. It looked rather like something that belonged in an aquarium. It also struck me as vaguely obscene.

I decided to remain seated and observe. There was no question about it: it was growing, and growing fast! Within half an hour that orange object had acquired the shape of a small, independent muscle with a little black cap on its top. When flies arrived and began to buzz around it and a curious smell reached my nostrils, it dawned on me that my visitor was probably some kind of stinkhorn. After an hour of uninterrupted vigilance it had doubled in size. I kept watching with intense fascination, and I swear I noticed very minor, almost imperceptible jerky movements, which were *not* caused by the flies. Up and up it pushed into the air, fearlessly thrusting aside a twig that blocked its way. By noon it had reached a length of four inches. It looked intriguingly alive and ready to crawl away at any given moment.

It did no such thing, of course, and it ceased to grow. The next day it had collapsed. It lay full length over the earth, motionless, like a big orange slug. But I was able to identify it: it was indeed a variety of stinkhorn. *Mutinus caninus,* says my field guide.

Others have come up since, though they were not always such spectacular growers. I now refer to them with a name of my own: *Fungus miraculus,* miracle mushroom. Because, as I have said, I believe in miracles. We take them for granted only too often, and I feel we ought to be reminded every now and then that miracles really do happen.

Cackling Cones

EVER SINCE MY EXPERIENCE with my evening primroses, I have been on the alert for possible other kinetic and vocal qualities in the kingdom of vegetation. Consequently I have discovered that certain representatives of our flora move even faster and have far louder voices than oenothera. This is the story of how yet another miracle (forgive me, I just can't get enough of these) revealed itself to me: the tale of the cackling cones.

I'm a dedicated pine cone fan, and pines and I have always been very close. My very first toy, so my mother told me, was a pine needle. I picked it up during a family picnic in the mountains above my native Monte Carlo, and I would not be parted from it. I have no memory of this event, but the needle is still in my possession: it is stuck, among other memorabilia, in an old album that my mother dedicated to me. It occupies the top left corner of a page, together with some faded black-and-white snapshots of the location of this very picnic. It is now brittle with age, and I fear that soon it will turn to dust altogether.

I must have been about seven when I first discovered how the weather influenced the scales of pine cones. When ripe, they open wide in the warmth, but they close again as soon as moisture is in the air. I immediately incorporated my own private cone into an already substantial collection of meteorological instruments: a discarded thermometer, accurate to about five degrees; a little wooden house with a weatherman and his wife, of which the latter was always out, rain or shine; a vial with shark oil given to me by a seafaring uncle who had bought it in Bermuda (the oil allegedly turns cloudy if bad weather is ahead); and, my most prized possession, a postcard with a girl in a magic dress, a dress that would turn pink during rain and blue in fine weather. The cone, however, very soon turned out to be the downfall of this collection, for when I found it to work only if exposed directly to the weather, I decided to transfer my entire workshop onto the sill outside the kitchen window, from where I felt my readings would be more accurate. And then, before the workshop could be noticed and salvaged by a grownup member of the family, a sudden downpour ruined the card, and the house, the vial, and the thermometer fell victim to the cat, who, trying to reclaim its territory, knocked them onto the stone pavement behind the house. Only the cone was saved. In a creative mood, I painted it gold, and for many years it was used as an ornament on our Christmas tree. I still have it.

Pine cones have never lost their charm for me, and I still rank them among nature's most fascinating designs. When I tramp through our local pine woods, I frequently find my path littered with quantities of cones. I cannot resist them, and whenever possible I collect a bagful (or two bags, if I have company to assist me). These I carry home like a precious hoard, and I find multiple uses for them. When their scales are open, I first shake them above a newspaper and collect their seeds, which whirl down in a peculiar spiraling motion caused by a single wing. These seeds are reserved as a very special treat for the birds and the squirrels. Next I toss the empty cones in a basket and keep them for the winter evenings, when they will be fed into the open fire and give me moments of sheer but short-lived ecstasy, for though they burn up very fast, it is only a matter of minutes before they have sent their intoxicating aroma of burning resin through the entire house.

Sometimes I select the largest and most perfect specimens and line them up on windowsills and bookshelves and above the fireplace. To the pragmatic mind this may not be one of the more useful pursuits in life, but I'm far from pragmatic, thank God, and the result is always most pleasing. I sit back and gloat over the fruits of my decorative inspiration, feeling like a hobbit in his cozy subterranean dwelling — though I shall never forget the day when a particular harvest of cones proved to house a colony of tiny bugs that emerged and fanned out over the walls and ceiling as soon as the cones were displayed in their usual locations.

Only very recently I discovered that, apart from having meteorological, ornamental, and odoriferous qualities, pine cones have more up their sleeve, or rather up their scales: they speak! Please don't laugh. And no, I don't want to hear any muttering from the back of the class. It is absolutely true: pine cones do have voices, which are sometimes quite powerful, though having them recite from the works of Milton or Dylan Thomas would, admittedly, be a trifle too much to ask. Neither do they sing Puccini arias.

It started with an invigorating walk in the rain one afternoon. I discovered a pine tree that had only recently been felled, and I noticed that its branches carried unusually large cones. They were not ripe yet, and their mahogany-colored scales were as tightly closed as the lips of prim virgins. Still, I decided to find out if they would ripen sufficiently to open up when put in a dry, warm spot at home, and I picked a bagful. (I never, ever leave home without at least one empty bag stuffed into my pocket.) Back at the cottage, I lined them up on the radiator in the kitchen and promptly forgot all about them.

In the middle of the night a strange sound woke me. Burglars, I thought. So I stayed in bed and waited for more sounds, meanwhile hoping for the right decision to mature in my mind. I received no inspiration, but yes, there was that sound again, and no, it might not be an intruder after all. It was an unusual noise, much like the explosion of a small firecracker. Then there was silence. And again an explosion. Good Lord, could something serious be the matter with the stove? I hopped out of bed and rushed into the kitchen, whence the sound came. The moment I entered there was another *bang!* but not at all from the stove. Then, near the radiator, something jumped on the floor. By now I more or less expected the patter of fleeing mice, or a marten, perhaps, for we have some unusual visitors in our region. But nothing could be heard. I walked over to the radiator, and as I bent over, again a loud *bang!* resounded, and simultaneously one of the pine cones flew up into the air and rolled onto the floor, where it joined three others.

My relief was immense. No burglars. No mice, which are almost as destructive. Just pine cones that opened their scales in the heat of the radiator, an abrupt process that was coupled with a curious exploding sound, while the sudden release of tension sometimes caused them to jump up and roll onto the floor. Though I rather liked this wonderful discovery, I gathered them all and put them outside the back door, for I feared the explosions might keep me awake during the rest of the night.

One golden afternoon early this season, I walked with a friend along my favorite track, which passes by a large old pine wood. It was a warm and windless day and even the birds had ceased to warble, as birds so often do during meridian hours. We trotted along in drowsy silence until suddenly we became aware of a mysterious cackling overhead, like a thousand tiny witches all gossiping at the same time. What on earth could it be? There was no wind, and neither could I discover a single bird or a frolicking squirrel touching the branches. We listened, we looked, we craned our necks until they ached, but no, nothing moved, and not a living creature was in sight. Yet something or other made itself heard. Then suddenly it dawned on me. The branches of that particular tree were crammed with small ripening cones. Hardly ever before had I seen such abundance in a single tree. And in the warm, dry air of that afternoon, thousands and thousands of scales were opening up, each of them producing a little cackling sound . . .

We sat down on an old and mossy trunk, my friend and I, and we listened for a while, for we both felt that during this unique performance the tree deserved a special audience.

Strictly Daffodils

I T WAS EARLY AUTUMN when I moved into the cottage, and already I had decided that the very first spring in my garden would have to be a very special one. A celebration of color, a staggering floral extravaganza. How I was going to achieve this, I had no idea whatsoever. It was to be my first garden in many, many years; I was a horticultural nitwit, and my knowledge was based mainly on experiences with pots of geraniums and petunias and aphid-ridden daisies on the balcony of my apartment. I did not worry. It was, after all, only October, and I had oceans of time to complete the order forms from stacks of nursery catalogues that littered my desk and gather additional information from a gardening book or two.

Of course it wasn't nearly as simple as that, and the first problem arose almost immediately: the ideal how-to garden book seemed nonexistent. Not that the booksellers failed to offer a choice. On the contrary, a maddening selection of books on a bewildering variety of topics crammed the shelves of the gardening sections. But not a single one answered all my questions. There were books on red roses. There were books on white lilies. Books with magnificent photos and no advice whatever. Books with intricate diagrams and designs for borders that would require the employment of a head gardener with a staff of at least ten to be laid out and maintained. Books on . . . well, the list goes on and on, and I became most depressed, and I gave up.

Instead I went to the children's section, in quite a different aisle, where I soon found a delightful book for my eight-year-old niece. It was about Easter bunnies, and it was charmingly illustrated. One picture in particular caught my eye: a couple of very intelligent-looking bunnies sitting in a field of daffodils under a blue sky. The bunnies were absolutely adorable, and the daffodils were . . . well, very much daffodils — forgive me if I sound silly, but that's the way it was. And suddenly I knew: there would have to be quantities of daffodils in my garden. Daffodils in the lawn. Daffodils in the borders. Daffodils peeking from under the hedge. Daffodils near the pond. I would assume the role of a floral Midas, and at my touch spring would turn into an orgy of gold all around the house.

You see, I have a secret fondness for daffodils. I can't think of a flower that flaunts a more essential yellow, that better symbolizes the spirit of spring, than the common, trumpet-brandishing daffodil. And yes, even the bunnies would be present, just as in the picture in my niece's book, because I had noticed some wild rabbit activity in my garden lately. They lived somewhere under the hedge, apparently, with a well-concealed entrance to their subterrestrial house on my side of the garden. Occasionally they hopped over the lawn, nibbling a little leaf here and a little blade of grass there and generally doing very little damage. Yes! Daffodils and bunnies, most definitely! I rushed home in a state of considerable excitement and began to pore over the latest bulb catalogues.

An hour or so later I was none the wiser for it, as I discovered that with daffodils it is as with books. Page after page of daffs in dozens of varieties. Tall ones and short ones. Orange ones. Some were too yellow, and some were too pale. Late-flowering ones. Highly recommended ones. "Our favorite choice" ones. Some looked like roses and some looked like weird spidery insects. Some looked like they ought to be psychoanalyzed. All of them had fancy names that sounded like wallpaper or cheap furniture from a sinister mail-order business, and their descriptions were richly peppered with the most monstrous adjectives. None looked like the straightforward, plain daffodil that I had in mind. Simplicity, it would appear, had become unfashionable. It was all too frustrating!

Finally I grabbed the telephone and dialed the number in the catalogue. A very friendly but somewhat mechanical-sounding lady answered my call.

"I want a specific variety of daffodil," I explained, "but I'm not sure if it is in your catalogue." Well, that was no problem, they had more in stock. What about variety X (I think it was called Morning Glory, or possibly Florida Sunset); the flowers were of a deep orange, almost red. No, that was not what I had in mind. I wanted ordinary yellow ones.

"Well, we have . . ." and here she proceeded to list about eight different varieties, none of which sounded like what I really wanted. The picture of my bunnies surrounded by a field of gently waving daffodils rapidly faded from my mind.

"Don't you have bunny daffodils?" I finally ventured in despair.

"Well, actually, we have a new variety that's rather fluffy in appearance. They're white and look very much like Jasmine . . ." Et cetera, et cetera.

This was impossible. I thanked the girl, hung up, and went to our local supermarket, where I knew there was the sweetest little garden section and a shelf with pre-packed bulbs. I was lucky. In a corner I found a stack of boxes with daffodil bulbs, in one variety only. They were modestly labeled DAFFODIL, with a simple colored illustration. Exactly what I wanted. I bought them all.

Let's skip the months that followed. The hours of labor involved in digging what seemed to be a million holes (in my eagerness I had bought far too many bulbs) and planting them, noses up, on a cold November morning. The suspense: would they come up? Had I planted them too deep? The frequent moments spent in front of the window, looking out into the desolate nakedness of winter, yearning for spring to come and trying to envision the garden with a multitude of daffodils nodding their heads in the breeze. Don't forget, it was my first year, and it was all new to me; I had not yet learned that patience is one of the prime ingredients in successful gardening.

And then all of a sudden it was late February, and the day was very mild, and the sun, though still low, caused instant activity in my garden's flora. Everywhere I noticed things sprouting and springing up, and countless green spears were diligently pushing through the dark soil and the still wintry-looking lawn: the daffodils were coming up! It could not be long now before they would burst into bloom, before the very first trumpet would herald spring.

Alas, they were doomed! Before they even had a chance to form buds they fell victim to the rabbits, who displayed an unexpected and unequaled voracity.* True, I did nothing to prevent this disaster. When one sees a tribe of baby bunnies frolicking about over the lawn, one is quite unable to deny them their favorite tidbit. There is something infinitely endearing about the way they daintily nibble blade after blade of tender young spring-time greenery. It is only after they have gone to bed, their little bellies comfortably stuffed with the fruits of one's labor, that one tends to build up a certain amount of rage, and by then it is far too late to do something about it.

* Since I consigned this adventure to paper, there has been a certain amount of murmuring. Bunnies, I have been told over and over, don't eat daffodils. "Are you sure?" is my standard reaction. Yes, they are sure. I'm sure they are sure, of course, but all the same, it is very intriguing. Here are the facts: I planted what was to be a forest of daffodils, but they were all very clearly and beyond doubt nibbled away. I naturally blamed the rabbits, for I had detected no other form of life in my garden. Could it be that there stealthily sneaked about some unknown creature with narcissophagous tendencies? Could the packer conceivably have made some error and packed the wrong bulbs in the wrong box? This would have been easy for me not to notice, since I was at the very beginning of my gardening career and still unable to distinguish a tulip from a turnip.

Anyway, to this day no light has been shed on the matter, and frankly, I prefer to keep it this way. I like the idea of harboring mysteries in my garden.

But when one morning I badly sprained my ankle by stepping into a rabbit hole that had been dug overnight in the middle of the lawn, it was the last straw and I invited the rabbit man. I told him to get rid of the creatures. I also told him that I was a coward and that I did not want to know what method he would employ. I would simply pay him and go away for a few days, and when I returned I would expect my garden to be entirely bunny-free and bunny-proof. And indeed, when I came back there was rabbit-proof netting along the fence and all holes had been filled in.

One morning about a month later, when I was home recovering from a particularly nasty bout of the flu, my neighbor walked in with a huge bunch of daffodils, fresh from her own garden. It was not a very tactful gesture, of course, after my daffodilian debacle, and her offering should have been enough to evoke my most evil instincts, but since she is a good soul and her gift was obviously not calculated to have any such effect, I forgave her. Anyway, they were splendid, strong and healthy daffodils, still in their bud, with only a hint of yellow showing through their thin, papery bracts. She lovingly arranged them in my favorite vase, put them on the table, and left. ("No, thank you, no coffee today. I'm in a hurry.") I picked up a book and settled into the easy chair. After a while I heard a faint rustling on the other side of the room. It came from the daffodils, and I suspected that some crawly had inadvertently migrated in with the flowers and was now conducting an investigation of its own. However, from where I was seated I could not see any movement, and I did not pay further attention. Seconds later there was that rustling again — a curious, papery noise, almost like a whisper. Now I was convinced that it was caused by the wings of some insect. I got up and had a closer look, but no, I could not detect even a trace of arthropodal life. Yet again I heard a whisper, and somewhere among the flowers there was a mysterious stirring. Suddenly I knew: cherished by the warmth of the springtime sun filtering through the window, the buds were opening rapidly. One by one, sometimes three or four at a time, these oddly shaped little brown parcels split open with a soft whisper, timidly displaying miniature sunbursts of gold through the cracks and preparing themselves for a luminous love affair with the beams of the morning sun. I sat down again. Their whispering continued until the last bud had burst open. A soft and secretive murmur, as if to encourage me to be strong, and not to despair, and to try again. I told them yes, I would. Strictly daffodils again next year. *Sans* bunnies . . .

Of Mice and Boys

HOW VERY ODD: a peanut tiptoeing over the lawn and vanishing under the hedge. Gamboling pine cones, yes. Partying flowers, most definitely. But who on earth has ever heard of a perambulating peanut, unless, of course, it is related to the Mexican jumping bean?

All the same, there it was last night, a peanut, left over from the squirrels' dinner, speeding through the garden as if driven by some supernatural force. No, it was definitely not a trick of the light, for though dusk was rapidly gathering, the straw-colored shell was still clearly visible.

Not visible, however, was the tiny night-colored creature at the end of the peanut. I discovered this half an hour or so later. Again a peanut miraculously marched away to some unknown destination, though this time it was much harder to discern on account of the advancing night. Immediately I switched on the garden light. The peanut came to an abrupt halt, and a tiny shadow flitted away from it and disappeared under the hedge. Aha! Mice!

I bear no grudge against mice. I have never understood the urge to jump on a chair and utter ear-splitting shrieks as soon as one of our tiniest mammalian representatives puts in an appearance. On the contrary, I feel rather sorry for the poor creature whenever it is forced to behold such a scene. It must be a frightening experience indeed when all of a sudden a towering mass of living flesh elevates itself into the air and is transformed into a bellowing monster, when your only intention is to have a little harmless nibble at your favorite cheese in the cupboard, and maybe chew a tiny hole in a bag of rice and help yourself to a grain or two for dessert.

Before you conclude that I'm actively encouraging live performances of Beatrix Potter stories in my larder, let me assure you that mice are less than welcome within — or between — the walls of my house. I may have bats in my belfry, but a mouse in the house is out of the question. It's all right as long as they stay in the garden, though. I like being entertained on warm summer evenings by a family of field mice having a garden fête at the edge of the lawn. They play and frolic and so obviously enjoy life that I wouldn't dream of interrupting their moment of merrymaking. I do all I can not to disturb them. Which is extremely hard, for as soon as they detect only the slightest motion, they evaporate.

Under my roof, however, it's quite another matter, and already I have waged several wars, with various degrees of success. The First Mouse War started when I came home from a journey one day and found that the seams of the curtains in one of the bedrooms had been munched away beyond repair. This was intolerable, of course, and my first reaction was to address the perpetrators severely and tell them that they had been very naughty mice and would they please be so kind as to leave as soon as possible. But it occurred to me that this might not be a very effective method. So I reluctantly purchased two mousetraps and placed them, baited with choice pieces of Gouda, in the spare bedroom.

I did not derive great satisfaction from the fact that the next morning I found two lifeless little victims trapped under the merciless steel. But at least from that moment on all remained quiet on the rodent front, and to this day the new curtains have not sustained any damage.

Mouse War II began much later, when one night I woke up to the unmistakable sound of mouse activity behind the wall next to my bed. My banging shut them up immediately, but not for very long. The moment I was about to drop off, they resumed their festivities, and there was a repeat performance. This went on all night, and I knew it was time to put the mousetraps to use again.

However, this time I was not very successful. I had underestimated my unwelcome guests, and over and over I found empty traps, the cheese neatly nibbled away without even springing them. So I resorted to poison, a solution that I very much abhor, and that was the end of it. I had won another war.

I have no illusions, though. (Mouse) life goes on. The walking peanuts are the living proof of it. The enemy is advancing, and I'm now prepared for MW III.

Nevertheless, the very word *mouse* is enough to evoke sweet memories of a series of incidents during my young years. These concerned mainly white mice. What boy does not have, at one time or another during his school years, at least one caged pet mouse occupying prime space on the desk in his room? A practice which, by the way, should be encouraged in every family, for we cannot be too young to learn how to care for another living creature, and a mouse is a very easy start.

Ours was not a very mouse-tolerant household, however, and I kept mine secretly in a discarded soup tureen on the bottom shelf of my closet. Unfortunately, one of them managed to escape, and the next day I faced the task of having to explain a mysterious hole in one of my shorts. But otherwise they were completely tame and did not seem to mind being transported under my shirt or even in my pockets. Once I brought one with me to school and hid it in the bag of the girl sitting in front of me. When it emerged after a couple of minutes, the result was most satisfying, with half the class standing on the desks — mostly girls, I'm afraid, screaming their pig-tailed heads off. Thank God the teacher was as wise as she was formidable. After I had convinced her that the mouse had, on its own account, temporarily managed to escape my custody, she thanked me for bringing it to school and proceeded to teach us that life, especially in the shape of such a harmless little animal, was nothing to be afraid of. But the girl, my victim, was never entirely convinced of this. I still see her occasionally. And although she is now a grandmother, she still is very much the stand-on-a-chair-and-scream-when-you-see-a-mouse type. For which I fear I'm partly to blame.

And my mice? Well, they thrived and multiplied, as mice do, and before long their smell gave them away. I was firmly told to get rid of them, or else. So I presented them to a friend, who for a while kept them — in his closet.

There has been one other important mouse-related incident in my life, which took place shortly after the episode I have just described.

It came to pass during the school vacation, when I stayed with my grandmother. The days of dancing evening primroses lay well in the past, and my attention was now focused on what was going on elsewhere in the village. I befriended many a farmer, and my buddy and I would earn a nice extra income by offering our services collecting wasp-ridden windfalls in the orchards or weeding the front gardens of the farmsteads.

One day a farmer asked us if we were willing to catch mice. His field, he claimed, was riddled with their holes, and he promised us a dime for each rodent.

We were only too willing, for mouse catching was already one of our favorite pastimes. It was very easy, really. All you had to do was pour a little water into their holes, and out popped the entire family, after which our young and agile hands quickly prevented their further escape. But since wild field mice were quite unlike our familiar white pets and could not possibly be tamed, we usually turned them loose again.

We set out to the farmer's field armed with a large empty bucket and a jerry can with water. We went to work and had a ball, for never in our lives had we seen so many mice. By teatime the bucket was half filled with a solid mass of wriggling and jumping furry little bodies. Any more and their level would rise too high, allowing them to escape again. So we went back to receive our earnings, which we expected to be considerable. We found the farmer and his family — his wife and two daughters — peacefully gathered around the enormous table in the cozy kitchen. I stepped forward and proudly showed him the bucket. As he peeked into it, his face assumed an expression of intense disgust. Then he said, "I'll give you a buck. But y'll have to drown them yerself."

I was furious, not only at so flagrant a display of deceit (we had calculated that we had at least five dollars' worth of mice in that bucket) but also at our own ignorance, because the possibility that these poor little quadrupeds would be exterminated had never even entered our heads. At any rate, it was something I could not allow to happen.

"A dollar?" I said. "A dollar? Well, for a dollar you can drown 'em yourself!" And with these words I tipped the bucket over and poured its living contents over the tiled kitchen floor.

There was instant pandemonium. The three women turned pale with mounting hysteria, and in no time they were up on the large table, dancing a wild gavotte among cups and plates. They clutched their aprons and yelled blue murder. For a while it looked as if the farmer was going to join them, but he changed his mind. A wild look came into his eyes as he worked himself into a state of crimson fury. Then he charged us like a bull. Fortunately, we had one factor in our favor: true to a well-established farmers' custom, the locals kept their shoes outside the kitchen door and entered the house in their socks. This man would definitely have caught up with us if it were not for the fact that he forgot to don his clogs. As he was about to collar my buddy, he stepped on a sharp piece of stone, which left him dancing in place on one leg and allowed us to escape to safety.

This was my very last mouse encounter, and thereafter I gave up all dealings with these rodents. They, in contrast, have not abandoned me. They have found my peanuts, and soon, I fear, they'll find me again. But until then I'll let them have it their way. In spite of their destructive nature, I can't help finding them endearing little things, as long as they remain out in the open. And who knows, maybe they have now acquired enough wisdom to stay away from the house. I sincerely hope so, for slaughtering mice is not my favorite pastime. After all, a mouse is a mouse is only a little mouse.

Hedgehog Day

F EBRUARY SECOND is just around the corner, and people in Punxsutawney, Pennsylvania, are getting ready for Groundhog Day. We have no groundhogs in our area, but five years ago I began to celebrate a similar occasion of my own: I call it Hedgehog Day. However, unlike the woodchucks, who seldom participate in the fun and frequently have to face the wrong end of a barrel, my hedgehogs play a major part in these festivities. There is one drawback, though: one can never predict with any accuracy when exactly the hedgehogs will emerge from their long hibernal slumbers, and therefore my fête is very much an impromptu affair. As springtime is drawing near, I have to be on the alert for certain signs that precede this occasion: the first days of mild weather, the appearance of the season's first bugs, the unfolding of the first daffodils . . . But one day, all of a sudden, I know: the hedgehogs are back!

Before you join me at this merry event, let me tell you a thing or two about these endearing creatures of the night, for I fear that most of you have only fuddled notions of this animal from the Old World. And that is regrettable, because you cannot think of a lovelier companion to help you out with your bug and slug problems in the garden. You would never have to live through the agonizing experience of seeing all your young lettuce plants destroyed by slugs the very morning after you have planted them if only you had a hedgehog at your service. You would not have to walk down your garden path with extreme caution on a rainy morning in order to avoid a revolting "sqllluaschhhischhh!" (sorry, I don't know how else to spell it) under your boots, caused by stepping on these slimy plunderers: your friendly hedgehog would have dealt with them well before sunrise. And believe me, once you have been face to snout with one of these charmers, your life will seem incomplete without them.

Please, do not misunderstand me. Hedgehogs are *not* domestic animals, though in my enthusiasm I may have conveyed this impression. They are essentially wild creatures, protected by law in many countries, but they happen to have little fear of people. Tempting though it may be to keep them as pets, they should be left alone, for they have little chance of happiness and health if kept in confinement. I apologize for elaborating on these details, but I have made a horrible discovery: hedgehogs have turned up in certain pet shops recently. For anything between $250 and $350, one can become the owner, and possibly the exterminator, of one of these clumsy little clowns. If my warning has come too late and you already have a prisoner pathetically scurrying about in a glass cage, I can only hope that it will be lucky enough to escape and meet a companion that was equally lucky, so that together they may start a hedgehog population in your area too (provided you live in the country).

I have had a long association with hedgehogs, but how well I remember my first encounter, at the age of six. An early morning, and I was still in bed. The milkman had just been along and deposited our daily ration of four bottles on the doorstep, next to my bedroom. Suddenly I heard the clink of a falling bottle, and I rushed out of bed, prepared to chase away a notorious milk thief, our neighbor's mischievous cat. However, when I peeked out the window, I beheld the strangest creatures I had ever set eyes on: four living pincushions, a large one and three baby ones, with pointed, gnomelike snouts. They were huddling around the broken bottle, merrily lapping up a puddle of milk.

I should immediately have been reminded of the doings of Mrs. Tiggy-Winkle, but since the works of Beatrix Potter had not found their way to my bookshelf, I knew nothing of hedgehogs. I had never even seen one. So I naturally arrived at the only possible conclusion: these prickly intruders were trolls! I uttered the loudest of shrieks and promptly woke up the entire household. My mother entered the room in a state of alarm, and I tried to explain what I had just witnessed. I fear that in my excitement, my imagination ran wild, and she must have concluded that I had been subject to a nightmare. She did look out the window, though only to please me, but the trolls, of course, had taken a French leave.

The next morning they were back, but this time I was wise enough to keep silent. I sneaked out of bed and woke up my mother, begging her to come and have a look at the trolls. She followed me, still half asleep, and sure enough, the entire troll family was still there, gathered around the spilled milk. Then my mother burst into a fit of girlish laughter. She sat down on the edge of my bed, and speaking in hushed tones close to my ear, as though she were imparting some fascinating secret, she told me all there was to know about hedgehogs, and how smart they were to knock over a bottle deliberately in order to get at the milk. But henceforth the milkman was instructed to leave the bottles on the windowsill, because Mother had other plans for her milk, and besides, well she knew that milk is not a healthy sustenance for the hedgehog's little stomach.

When I moved to the country, it did not take me long to discover that we had a nice little hedgehog colony in our neighborhood. Since I had no dog (which is one of the hedgehog's very few natural enemies), they soon developed a marked preference for my garden, and they have been around ever since. On warm summer nights I sit on my terrace and they never fail to put in an appearance, sometimes as many as four or five at a time. They run around the house. They play and they fight. They hiss like tiny steam engines, and they make love — very carefully, of course. They scurry noisily through the borders and generally make their presence very well known without being in the least disturbed by mine. On the contrary, as the season advances, they choose to ignore me altogether, and once I had the honor of having a courting couple shuffle right over my feet! I do reward them, though, and lure them closer with peanuts (unsalted!), which they absolutely adore. Not too many, of course, lest they should become lazy and neglect their duty of slug munching and bug catching.

Peanuts too are essential to determine their return in early spring: as soon as winter has breathed its last breath of frost, I put some peanuts in the shell in a sheltered spot in the garden. If in the morning they are all gone without a trace, I know it was not a hedgehog who feasted on them. But if I find an unmistakable mess of empty shells, the word goes out immediately: the hedgehogs are awake! As soon as the weather permits I proclaim Hedgehog Day, and that very night I invite friends and neighbors, all of whom are hedgehog devotees. We sit in the garden wrapped in blankets, because in early spring the nights are seldom mild. For the hedgehog there is an extra helping of peanuts, about ten feet away from us. We keep our whispered conversation to a bare minimum, because our guest of honor will still be a little shy, and we don't want to disturb him. Meanwhile I see to it that there is an ample supply of mulled claret, which helps to keep us warm and adds to the festive mood of this important day.

The events always follow a predictable course: no sooner has darkness set in than there is a mysterious scuffling and scrambling under the bushes, and before long the hedgehog emerges from the shadows and ventures into the ring of light from the garden lamp. He ignores us, zigzags his way toward the peanuts, and proceeds to attack without delay, quite forgetting his table manners. After the last peanut has been munched away he does an about-face and heads for the pond for a noisy slurp of water, much to the distress of the frogs — especially the smaller ones, who know well that they might become part of his banquet if they're not careful.

When finally the performance of our spiny comedian is over (he has never yet disappointed us by canceling his visit) and he has vanished into the darkness beyond the hedge, we retire, groggy with wine and sleep. Hedgehog Day is over. But spring, with its glorious promise of new life, has definitely arrived.

Rhapsody in Yellow

I F ONE IS TO BELIEVE the almanac, it is easy to distinguish one season from another. It rigidly divides the year into four equal parts; on the twenty-first of March, winter simply slinks away and in comes spring, tripping like a prima ballerina through our gardens. Nature, however, sublimely ignores these calendric hints and frequently neglects to indicate a clear borderline between the two. An unusually mild day in January's tail never fails to trick the birds into a feeble and premature Jubilate, whereas I remember occasions on which the daffodils sported idiotic coiffures of snow as late as April.

But last year spring literally, and miraculously, "happened" overnight, and of course it was *not* on March twenty-first. What is more, it happened exclusively in and around our village. We woke up one morning in April and found that spring had spread her golden cloak over us, and . . .

And here I should leave spring alone for a while and take you back in time — back to that infamous October gale of the previous year. For almost twenty-four hours it raged, snapping trees as if they were matchsticks, howling around our chimneys, blowing shingles off our roofs. A particularly strong gust forced a lonely truck off the narrow road outside our village. The driver momentarily lost control of his wheel and down he dived into the shallow ditch. The truck toppled over, its tarpaulin tore open, and its contents spilled out: a load of tiny black grains. These whirled up in the wind in grotesque sweeps and swirls, farther and farther away over the wintry fields and the entire village. They danced in clouds through the yards and somersaulted over the roofs. They spiraled over the streets and pirouetted in miniature tornadoes around the church. And what by then had not yet settled down vanished in reveling wisps over yet more fields beyond, to destinies unknown.

Meanwhile the driver, who had escaped without a scratch, sounded the alarm to some local farmers. They arrived at the disaster area with a small armada of tractors and jeeps and vans. With their dark coats flapping in the wind, they looked like a colony of strange huge birds while they relentlessly toiled away with chains and ropes. Finally they managed to pull the truck onto its four wheels and tow it out of the ditch. Apart from the torn tarpaulin and some minor dents, it had very little damage. Its load was gone, however. Not a single grain was left. The wind had generously scattered it over the village and all the surrounding fields and woods.

It had by no means been a dramatic incident. There were no casualties, and after the truck had gone there was not a shred of evidence left to betray that anything had happened at all. Nothing more was thought of it. The event didn't even make it to the pages of our local paper, and it soon fell into oblivion altogether.

Not only was the winter cold and wet, it was also one of the longest I have ever endured. The soggy fields lay bleak and bare under the heavy skies, and the conditions of my favorite walk through the dripping woods were appalling; most trails had been reduced to streams of mud that mercilessly sucked at one's boots and made it almost impossible to advance. Consequently, my outings were strictly limited to short strolls to and from the village and an occasional inspection tour in my garden. Other than that, I stayed at home most of the time, while the world hung in tears on the windowpanes and the rain pitter-pattered on the roof like the feet of a thousand crows.

No wonder that by the end of February I was plunged

into the very deepest state of gloom. So, I'm sure, was our flora. The absence of young green was truly frightening, and unexpected spells of frost all through the month of March discouraged and delayed all fresh sprouting activities. But nature cannot be stopped, and eventually a thin veil of frostbitten green spread over trees and shrubs. The first weeds carefully pushed through the sodden earth, and a few late snowdrops timidly flirted with some limp crocuses. But it was all rather pathetic. It lacked the usual spirit of the season, and for once I had to force myself even to feign interest in the goings-on outside the house. Even some strange weeds, never before seen in my garden, did not arouse my curiosity; nor did the fact that these same weeds manifested themselves on the roof of my little toolshed and sprang up hither and yon between the cobblestones of our lanes, in the cracks of our main street's sidewalk, and in numerous other unexpected nooks and crannies. The days were simply too wet to pay attention to such trivialities. I hurried along on my necessary errands, eager to get back under the shelter of my roof as soon as possible.

But all the while true spring was waiting around the corner, secretly calculating its moment of triumph. One afternoon there was a sudden change in the weather. The skies cleared up, and in my pool-riddled lawn there were unexpected reflections of azure and gold. Myriads of diamonds sparkled in an almost blinding symphony of light, and a mild southerly breeze breathed instant life into the long-suffering verdure. Finally springtime had made her entrée. The effect was astonishing. Everything seemed to happen at once. Buds were swelling and bursting into life within two days. Weeds grew faster than they could be pulled out, and the strange intruders in particular flourished with exceptional diligence. One could almost hear them grow. Meanwhile I had recognized them as rapeseed (a kind of mustard cultivated for its oil), but their origin was a dark mystery to me. No amount of leftover birdseed could possibly account for this enormous invasion. They didn't look offensive, though. On the contrary, their bluish green leaves and stalks appeared succulent and possessed some undeniable charm. Once in bloom with their clusters of small bright yellow flowers, they might even look pretty, I thought, and I decided to let most of them stay, for a while at least.

It was my neighbor across the road who shed light on the enigma of their origin, though at first I misunderstood her.

"'Tis Thexident," she stated one morning, leaning on my garden gate and allowing her eyes to wander casually around my garden in the hope of finding something to disapprove of. Like most gardeners, she couldn't abide to see anything thrive in other gardens that didn't do well in her own, with the exception of weeds, of course, like this invasion of rapeseed. She also had a peculiar habit of endowing plants with corrupted names. Thus she would call zinnias "cynthias" and hydrangeas "hystrangleas." I was usually able to reconstruct her maimed nomenclature, but "Thexident" baffled me. I had a momentary vision of some new brand of toothpaste, but she was obviously referring to the mustard.

"Oh," I muttered, "I thought it was rapeseed."

"That's what I said. All that rapeseed. 't happened after thexident, when all them seeds blew all over the place."

It dawned on me. But of course! She was referring to last year's accident, when that truck blew off the road and lost its load of tiny grains. It had never occurred to me that those had been rapeseeds. They had lain dormant all winter long, blending in with the dark, wet soil, and everybody had forgotten about them. When finally they began to sprout, in early spring, they were simply ignored and left to grow, because it was far too wet to do any gardening. They would have to wait until the world became a little drier again. Today was such a day, but being a regular working day, few people found time for gardening, and the maintenance schedule of the communal grounds — the streets, the village square, the church, and so on — did not allow for such unplanned activities as pulling weeds out of sidewalks. And so this rapeseed continued to thrive, undisturbed, throughout the area.

The miracle of spring happened the very next day. I felt the promise of another glorious morning the moment I woke up, but little was I prepared for the spectacle that I was about to behold. As soon as I opened the curtains, yellow leapt into view from every window. Not just the yellow of the bright morning sun, unless the sunbeams had metamorphosed into solid matter (which, now I come to think of it, was probably what had happened). Miraculous clouds of solid sunlight were hovering over my entire garden. Everywhere I looked there were wafts of golden yellow. In the lane beyond the gate and between the trees too, the powerful vibration of this golden haze greeted me. Evidently, after the blessing of the sun during these last few days, all the rapeseed had burst into bloom simultaneously, as though in a secret pact to conquer even the light of the sun.

I forgot about breakfast. I forgot about work. There were more important things that needed my immediate attention: outside waited another miracle to be investigated.

As soon as I was dressed I hurried into the garden. Yellow was rampant. It gleamed all around the house. It crowned the toolshed. And, oh dear, a single plume shimmered even on top of the chimney, like the crest of a cockatoo. I wandered into the lane. Here too spring danced its gay gavotte of yellow. I walked toward the village and marveled at the yellow streaks that flew like broad golden streamers over the fields I passed. On the village green I encountered an unusual crowd. People looked around in silence, unbelieving. Here too yellow magic had been splashed about with a liberal brush. It radiated in the most unexpected corners — in the gutters of the terraced houses, in the lap of the Maria statue near the home for the aged, and even on the roof of the ancient church, where it quivered like a strange aureole that had somehow lost its saint.

It was nothing short of a miracle. In one night our world had been framed in gold. The village had been transformed into a giant painting, and from His palette the Master had chosen yellow to sign His latest work of art.

Country Callers

A VISITOR, to many of us, is a relation, a friend, *belle Maman,* a neighbor, the parish priest. They arrive, sometimes unannounced and not always at a convenient moment. Nevertheless, we park them on our favorite chair and politely offer them some beverage, which we hope will be declined. It usually isn't. In short, they may not always be welcome, yet the moment they cross our threshold they become our visitor, our guest, and we observe certain rules that are as ancient as humanity. There are exceptions, of course, though I would go too far to say who, or what, these exceptions exactly are. The laws of hospitality are unwritten, and it is very easy to observe them at our own convenience. One of *my* laws, for instance, is, or rather was, that I did not tolerate unannounced or unexpected visitors. When one lives in the city, leading a hectic urban life, and one's diary is crammed with punctiliously timed obligations, an unexpected ringing of the doorbell can easily lead to total disruption of one's plans. I'm sure my attitude was not unique, for I believe that the majority of people in metropolitan areas don't bother to answer their bell unless they are absolutely sure whom to expect on the other side of the door.

But when I left the city and went to rusticate in my present abode in the country, I soon found that I had to change my attitude toward visitors. And not only that: I had to alter my entire conception of the meaning of hospitality. Everything about it was different. A front door, for instance, seemed absurdly superfluous. No one ever used it except myself, and only during the first couple of weeks. After that it remained permanently locked, and I lost the key, and all traffic became strictly a back-entrance affair. Prearranged arrivals were virtually nonexistent; not only did the majority of callers appear totally unexpectedly, a quick rat-tat-tat on the kitchen door being their only warning, they also seemed to consider some parts of the house "open to the public." Thus I was frequently startled by the sudden appearance, in the corridor or in the kitchen, of a friendly neighbor bearing some gift: a basket of homegrown tomatoes, French beans, or strawberries, a tin of home-baked cookies, or a plate of pound cake, still warm from the oven and usually weighing at least twice its name.

At first I found it hard to cope with these trespassing villagers and their gifts. I could not help feeling like a Buddhist priest in Bangkok, accepting offerings from dutiful worshipers. Before long, however, I began to adjust to the doings of rural life and learned to view these neighborly intrusions in their true light: as spontaneous expressions of respect for one's fellow beings, combined with a healthy dose of curiosity (often ill concealed) and a need for harmless gossip. I also learned an additional rule: one was always expected to return basket, tin, and plate, preferably containing some produce of one's own.

Of all the visitors to whom I offered the shelter of my roof, one in particular stands out in my memory, for several reasons. First, he entered the room in an unorthodox manner: through an open window. Second, he was my very first visitor, arriving only hours after I had moved in. And third, he was not human. It all began like this:

After a session of frantic unpacking, I was relaxing with a cup of strong Assam tea at the large table in the dining room when I detected some movement in the living room. I peeked around the corner, and yes, there he was, in my favorite chair. Well, not actually *in* it; rather, he was perched on the very top of its back. He was a brownish red, furry little creature with comical plumed ears and a long bushy tail elegantly curled upward. As soon as he noticed me, he froze. So did I. For more than a minute we stared at each other, and I hardly dared to breathe, lest I should disturb him. This was too good to be true: my very first day in the country, and already a red squirrel had honored me with a visit. I doubted, though, if my presence was equally appreciated: he observed me, and I read a mixture of curiosity and suspicion in his beady little eyes. Then he turned around, gracefully leaped onto the windowsill, and vanished through the open window into the garden. Never to be seen again, I thought; it had been but an investigative call, and my presence must have disturbed him.

How wrong I was, for the next day he was back. This time he did not surprise me, for I had already noticed him in the garden, frolicking about among the branches of the tall conifer on the side of the house. Suddenly he jumped onto the sill and from there onto the carpet. His intention was immediately obvious: he had designs on a bowl of peanuts that I had put aside for the titmice. Like countless other items, it sat on the floor, most tabletops and chairs still being entirely occupied by the contents of recently unpacked boxes and crates. Stealthily he crawled nearer and nearer. He snatched one of the nuts with his mouth, quickly readjusted it into a comfortable position with his front paws, and scampered back into the garden, where he buried his treasure under the hedge. Within seconds he was back. He now made a beeline for the bowl — already he seemed to know his way around — and another peanut was soon buried in the garden, under the hydrangea bush this time. He kept coming back, and within half an hour the bowl was empty.

From that day on he became one of my regular visitors. Every morning he put in an appearance and demanded breakfast — peanuts usually, but occasionally I was in an extravagant mood and would treat him to hazelnuts, which stand number one on a squirrel's menu. Sometimes the window was closed, for in our northern clime one simply cannot keep windows open at all times, but he refused to take no for an answer. Furiously he would jump up against the windowpanes, covering them from top to bottom with muddy paw prints. I was usually too weak-hearted to deny him access, and inevitably the result was an icy living room, which meant extra sweaters, sometimes even an overcoat, and cups of hot cocoa, and an ever-increasing heating bill, for the window had to be left open until his departure. This practically forced me to the obvious solution: the installation of a special squirrel door, which is very much like a cat door in the window. Oh yes, it looks awful, and it is unlikely to find its way into the pages of fashionable interior design magazines, but one must make certain concessions for the sake of one's visitors, especially for such exalted beings as red squirrels.

Squirrels are not my only guests. Frequently birds decide that an open window or an open door means open house and "help yourself to whatever is available." My regulars now include an adult male blackbird, a peculiarly inquisitive robin, an escaped parakeet (I have never been able to trace its owner), and several species of titmice, of which the great tits are the most audacious. Not only do they come in to hunt for titbits, they also go after my furniture, or at least parts of it. That first year they appreciated the soft upholstery of one of my chairs, and in the course of a week they had pecked a hole in it, hysterically digging for fluff and lint, which they carried off to their own homes to line their nests. Last year they developed a penchant for my red tartan throw. It became practically the sole building material for one of their nests, as I found out at the end of the season, when I cleaned out their house and found it entirely stuffed with red woolen fluff.

By then my list of nonhuman visitors had become quite exceptional, and in order to keep track of each of these important events, I began to mark them down in my diary. Thus, if one turned, for instance, to May 17, one would read, "9:00 A.M., squirrel (steals apple pie); 12:30, luncheon with Mr. & Mrs. Smith; 4:30 P.M., crested tit comes to tea!" I wonder what the Smiths would think of me should they read this. They might not like being squeezed in between squirrels and crested tits. They might consider me somewhat unbalanced, and they might never ask me to lunch again. They can't be blamed, though, for they live in a big city, on the eighth floor, and they don't know any better. I feel sorry for them, for their only appointment with nature is limited to an occasional stroll through a city park, where their children may feed some already overfed pigeons or dowdy ducks that languidly float about in manmade ponds.

I'm infinitely more privileged. Nature always has an appointment with me. Her children honor me by calling on me in my own home. And in this age of stress and ever-increasing violence, there is a lot of healing and peace in their calls.

Paradise Lost

THE WRENS are no more. Gone is their cozy, well-concealed nest in the dense honeysuckle against the house next door. Gone too are their nine eggs, tiny white gems with spots of crimson. Gone is the blackbird's home with its three babies, on the other side of the house. Indeed, gone is the entire garden! All fell victim to man's greed and uncontrollable lust for order. Because the old lady died.

She had been ill and away for so many years that hardly a soul remembers what she looked like. I certainly don't, for I never set eyes on her. Not once since I moved into my cottage five years ago did I see her, nor anyone else, in or around her house. No milkman and no post-man, no plumber and no sweep. Never a gardener. The house stood completely abandoned, an entity hiding in the privacy of its own wilderness, a jungle that became a little more impenetrable each year.

"How can you stand living next to such a dump?" I have been asked frequently. "All those *weeds!*"

"I manage somehow," I usually answer, shrugging my shoulders and assuming a fake expression of resignation. It is useless to argue, and I prefer to keep the secrets of that "dump" to myself. Believe it or not, it actually shares its mysteries with me and liberally sheds its welcome floral gifts through and over the hedge into my garden. It endowed me with a patch of lilies of the valley; they sent their rhizomes under the hedge and came to life in my border. A huge rhododendron could not contain its curiosity and boldly thrust its branches through the hedge in order to observe the goings-on in my garden. In four years' time these branches have developed into a seemingly independent rhododendron bush, and this year they bloomed with a breathtaking extravaganza of pinkish lilac. Pink and dark purple garden balsam have shot their seeds high over the hedge into my soil, and every July and August they transform a remote corner of my border into a small paradise for swarms of bumblebees. These drone about the livelong day and busily wriggle their furry little bodies deep into the hearts of these lovely flowers, shaped very much like small orchids. Weeds indeed!

I remember the very first time I ventured through the disintegrating wooden gate and, in search of secrets and surprises, penetrated into this miniature jungle. The small house was almost invisible. Dense masses of polygonum (knotweed, but I find more poetry in the old-fashioned name, mountain fleece) covered an entire wall of this single-story dwelling. The other side, including the front door, lurked behind a heavy growth of luxurious honeysuckle, which sent its heavenly fragrance far into the neighborhood (on warm summer evenings it frequently wafted through my open windows, mingling with moths and mosquitoes). The remainder of the structure, most of the windows included, was obscured by common ivy and Virginia creeper.

It wasn't the house, however, that aroused my curiosity. What immediately captured my attention was the remarkable tangle of countless shrubs, the soft carpet of leaves and thick, voluptuous mosses, the numerous weeds and wildflowers (tell me, what *is* the difference?) in what I presumed had once been the lawn. Somewhere in a corner I made a wonderful discovery: a jasmine and a rose embraced each other in a floral love affair. They had become one. I suppose it was the jasmine who encroached on the rose's territory, for the rose was clearly the older. It certainly was the tallest rose I had ever seen, with thorny branches almost as thick as my arm. But it had tolerated the intruder, and now its delicate pink flowers freely mingled with a cascade of snowy white jasmine blossoms.

Needless to say, this undisturbed corner of our neighborhood had enticed its own wildlife population. It became a favorite hangout for local blackbirds. I counted at least a dozen old nests, and a new one, occupied by a sitting blackbird hen. A thrush had built her home in the wrought-iron lamp at the back door, and a robin flew in and out through a small broken window of what I think might have been the bathroom. There was some scurrying on the ground too — mice, I believe, though the creatures were too fast to allow proper identification, and toads so lazy that I had to be careful not to tread on them. At nighttime I often heard the unmistakable noise of rummaging hedgehogs, those lovable creatures of the night about whom I told you in an earlier chapter. I think they lived there, and even hibernated there in their safe underground winter residence. And this spring a couple of wrens joined the crowd and declared in shrill notes that the honeysuckle was theirs. They built a nest in it, an ingenious affair of moss, almost invisible.

And now the old lady has passed away. The house will be put up for sale. Apparently, though, it was decided that the dwelling's present state would not do and would render it undesirable to prospective buyers. It must be made presentable.

And so one morning last week the men came. They brought with them their tools of trade and started their work without further ado. From morning till evening the air was filled with deafening sounds of sawing and grinding, of laughter and loud radios, and by five o'clock they were done. Nothing had been spared. Not the patch of lilies of the valley. Not the trees and the shrubs. Not the jasmine and the rose. Not even the rhododendron. All had been pulled up. Destroyed. Obliterated. The climbers had been ripped off the walls. The whole plot had been plowed and turned into a naked patch of soil, without so much as a single blade of grass.

I could not help thinking of the agony this transformation must have caused among its local population. What had happened to the wrens that had lived in the honeysuckle? To the blackbirds and the thrushes? The families of mice and shrews and hedgehogs that must have had their cozy dens somewhere below the ground? The peaceful toads who had their shelters under stones and logs? In fewer than eight hours their little heaven had been turned into hell. Their world had come to an end.

As for the house, it is now visible from afar. Its windows, many more than I had thought, stare out at me like sad eyes. I stare back, equally sad. All I see is a bleak and forlorn structure with scarred, naked walls, utterly alone in its desolate solitude. A property that must be turned into cash as soon as possible. Paradise, it would appear, could not do that. Paradise, for which we are always looking. Yet, sadly, sometimes when it's there, we do not see it.

Paradise Found

NATURE IS TOO POWERFUL to be permanently obliterated. However fierce a brushfire rages across the land, the very next spring the blistered earth will split open above roots and rhizomes and young green will eagerly sprout up, pretending that nothing happened at all. Fireweed will appear from nowhere and occupy its new territory with its signature of powerful pinkish purple. Birds will be back, contributing to the recovery of their territory by dropping seeds and berries from elsewhere. Rabbits will return and tunnel their way into their old warrens.

No, destruction never lasts. Since ancient times volcanic eruptions have obliterated towns, yet before long the inhabitants usually return to their land and rebuild their houses on the charred remains of the old dwellings. Be it plant or bird, beast or man, the phoenix always rises from the ashes.

Man-inflicted destruction too is often a temporary matter, if only nature is left to follow its course, or assisted to do so. So I should not have worried too much when in a single day ruthless workmen turned the deserted garden next to mine into a total wasteland. But at the time I couldn't see it that way. It was simply awful: not a sprig of green was left. All the coppice, the intriguing tangle of roses and jasmine and elder, had been obliterated, including their population of blackbirds and thrushes and robins and wrens. Even the hedge that separated our gardens had to succumb, and suddenly I was granted a desolate vista of nothing but naked soil. Moreover, it meant that my garden too was stripped of its protection and rudely exposed to the curious gaze of all and sundry. No doubt some form of vegetation would one day return, but for the moment I might just as well have been sitting on the pavements of Manhattan. No wonder I was in the doldrums.

After a week of sulking indoors, with the curtains on that side of the house permanently drawn in spite of a glorious summer, I decided to do something about it. I lost no time, and before the clock struck the hour of noon I had erected a temporary six-foot fence made of rush matting. It looked natural and unobtrusive and instantly restored the intimacy on my side of the world. Since this was not meant to be a permanent solution, my next step would be to plant a hedge, but that would have to wait until the fall.

The following morning I opened all the curtains and celebrated my regained independence with an elaborate breakfast in the garden, without anyone's being able to count the eggs on my plate (which were more than my regular diet allows).

Peace did not last; it never does. Within a week a representative of the local authorities stood on my doorstep, demanding to see a building permit. Since building, in my opinion, is related to bricks, I assumed he referred to a very low experimental wall I had constructed in a corner of the garden, with vague ideas of filling it up with soil and creating a rock garden. I was not too pleased with the result, and already I had decided to remove it. It was therefore without much pain that I promised to take it down as soon as possible.

Three days later I received a letter in the mail. From the authorities. Much to their regret, they had noticed that I had ignored their instruction to pull the wall down. They gave me two more days, or else . . .

This was absurd, infuriating. What wall? Did they want me to pull my house down? I waited until I had worked myself into a proper paroxysm of anger before I went to pay a personal visit to the authorities.

A green-livered unknown authority with an osseous smile received me, and during the somewhat heated discussion that ensued, it became clear that they had referred to the fence. This, of course, was sheer lunacy. I tried to explain that I had not built a wall but only erected a screen, and a temporary one at that, in order to protect my paradise against their hell. Admittedly, this was not a very nice thing to say, since the authorities were not the owners of the adjoining property and therefore not in the least responsible for its present state, but I fear that I suffered from a *crise de nerfs* and could therefore not be blamed for what I said. Next I explained that the separation was all natural, hardly more than tall dry grass in winter, and who could possibly object to it? Well, *he* did, and his grin became even more osseous as he proceeded to inform me that it was against local regulations to erect any kind of partition over three and a half feet high without a permit.

After I had made sure that it was not against local regulations to plant a hedge — it was not, of course, even if I decided to let it grow to a height of thirty feet — I left, as furious as I had come. I immediately wrote a letter to the very highest authority, stating that the natural components of my separation had unexpectedly developed roots and were starting to grow. It had therefore legally become a hedge, and in view of the local regulations I was under no obligation to take it away. This, of course, was a howling lie if ever there was one, and I did not expect anyone to believe it. Soon, I feared, they would be back, with a demolition team to pull down my helpless fence, after which they would probably arrest me. However, mysterious are the ways of the powers that be, and I heard nothing more of it.

The fence, by the way, did not last very long. Shortly after the autumnal equinox a gale blew it to shreds, and two days later I planted the new hedge.

Meanwhile there had been a coming and going all summer long of prospective buyers of the property. Until one day the FOR SALE sign was gone. I had new neighbors!

I didn't altogether trust them at first. It seemed to me that whoever decided to acquire such a desolate plot must be of an atrabilious disposition and acutely deprived of imagination, if not all senses. It didn't occur to me that it could well be the opposite. Yet it was soon evident that the new occupants, an elderly couple, had more than an average dose of imagination. From the very first day their garden was buzzing with activity. They were digging and raking and hoeing and planting from dawn till dusk. What struck me in particular was that they planted quantities of mysterious plants and saplings, most of which, it transpired, had been gathered during rambles through surrounding woods and fields. Apparently they preferred a wild flora to conventional squads of chrysanthemums and dahlias, and the thought occurred to me that the spirit of the old garden might still be hovering about and guiding their doings.

At times we had short, informal chats over the hedge, and I learned that they had exchanged the city for a country lifestyle for much the same reasons I had: to escape the hustle and bustle of cosmopolitan activity. He had retired and hoped to spend the remainder of his days in rural tranquility. He loved gardening, and he had selected this particular site for its location as well as for its bareness, which offered him the opportunity of a fresh start. Not that he had anything spectacular in mind; on the contrary, his intention was to let nature do its own work as much as possible. No more nice, velvety lawns, he stated, but instead a miniature meadow. Lots of bushes and trees — that would give the birds a chance . . . By the way, he loved my garden. So many secret nooks and corners.

Generally I'm not interested in my neighbors' doings and opinions, since they usually differ from my own, but this sounded like music to my ears. I immediately recognized my stroke of good luck, for shared opinions in such matters as gardening are infinitely more valuable than, let us say, a mutual political interest. Politics is strictly an indoor affair, whereas our two gardens were physically connected and could therefore greatly influence each other. It also meant that henceforth I could safely abandon all frantic efforts to blot his garden entirely from my view. Though it would probably never grow back to its original state of neglect, some of its jungly chaos might be restored under the careful supervision of its new owners, and more birds, more wildlife, more flowers might once again find a safe haven.

Which, I'm happy to say, is exactly what happened. This spring the wrens returned and built their nest in the newly planted honeysuckle, which last summer grew like mad. The small lawn in front of the house looked like a miniature meadow, where sprigs of grass loitered in a rich carpet spangled with buttercups and daisies and poppies and ground ivy. And a couple of audacious blackbirds built their nest in the still-transparent crown of the young chestnut tree.

One mild evening my neighbors invited me over to join them for after-dinner coffee on their flowery lawn. At one moment during a flag in our conversation, I noticed the man looking around his garden with unconcealed fondness. It is of a modest acreage and still in its infancy, but it seemed as though he looked into the future and with a mental eye perceived the promise of a small Shangri-La.

"You know," he said, out of the blue, "I've always wanted to live in paradise. I think I've found it."

Gnomes

W HAT SECRET FORCE, I often wonder, induces some people to populate their gardens with plaster gnomes in such aggressive colors that even the brightest flowers will look startled and some- what pale? Begonias will begin to sulk, petunias will develop inferiority complexes, and geraniums will ap- pear slightly anemic. Yet some such mysterious compul- sion must have worked in the minds of one of my neigh- bors; a swift glance over their garden gate will certainly confirm this. One's eye is immediately caught by the Chief Gnome, dominating the center of the lawn with his wheelbarrow-load of scarlet geraniums. Scattered about are armies of lesser gnomes in various poses of labor, while five even lesser ones appear to have a fishing competition around the pond, accompanied by several giant bright green frogs.

"Say no more!" I can almost hear some of you mutter in agony, for you, like me, have little sympathy for these gaudy horrors. But should you ask me, "Do you *believe* in gnomes?" I'll only smile politely. I'll do my utmost to convey, without words, the impression that I tolerate your silly question. Then I'll tactfully try to change the subject.

At this point I must make a confession, and if you don't mind, I'll whisper it, because I don't want the whole world to hear this. To you, though, it won't come as a shock, since I already briefly mentioned it some-where in the previous pages: I myself have a Gnome Garden. Don't worry, though — you are unlikely to see a single visible gnome in it. I chose the name merely as insurance, just in case gnomes *do* exist (the contrary was never proved). And should they indeed be miracu-lous gardeners, as many a story claims, I hope they will be flattered and lured into my garden to work their miracles.

It is unlikely that outsiders will be the least bit im-pressed by my Gnome Garden, which is no more than a neglected and remote corner of the garden. It is a place where all things green and growing are welcome and where gatecrashers will not be turned away, provided there is room for them. I fear that to the eye of the serious gardener it holds little harmony. In other words, it is a mere wilderness of weeds. There are certain limits, of course, and even the gnomes may need a helping hand occasionally. Some weeds simply cannot be tolerated, not even by me, and it would be a lie to state that I don't get my share of these obnoxious intruders. On the contrary, in view of my green tolerance I probably get more than the neighboring gardens, whose owners immediately pull out the most diminutive green specks that can't be accounted for. At any given moment they are able to sum up their garden's entire inventory with infuriating accuracy, because *Ordnung soll sein,* and after having done so they will gloat and look at you like the cat that swallowed the canary. Not without reason, I hasten to admit, since it is indeed a great accomplishment to be a successful monarch in one's own plot. I, however, will never, ever be able to achieve this. Which is probably just as well, because I don't want to. I prefer uncertainties, surprises. So, I'm sure, do the Little People, if they exist, and I try very hard to believe that some of my garden surprises are gnome-related, for the idea pleases me, and it keeps me out of mischief.

Take the red campion, for instance, which appeared without an invitation, tactfully selecting the one spot where it could flaunt its flowers to their best possible advantage and where it could misbehave and cause incidents. Like last year, when one of the villagers stopped by for a chat over the garden gate. During our entire conversation she glanced continually in a certain direction somewhere behind my left shoulder, until she could no longer contain her curiosity. "What are those lovely pink flowers?" she asked. I turned around and saw what she meant: towering above some ferns near the hedge were the flowers of the campion. They introduced such an unexpected flash of color into this dark corner that they created the illusion of something wildly exotic. But as soon as I informed her that they were campions, she flinched, and her gaze of admiration was promptly switched off. "But those are *weeds!*" she gasped. She made the word *weeds* sound as though it were some obscure disease. I sort of lost control. Silly woman. Why should a flower cease to be beautiful the moment it is named?

"Yes," I snapped, "they're weeds, and very beautiful ones into the bargain, and they're not only pink but white as well." And as an afterthought I added, "The gnomes planted them!" It was out before I knew. Poor soul, no wonder she looked startled; she had suddenly discovered that I was not only colorblind but slightly mad as well.

"Well, ta-ta, won't keep you!" she muttered hastily, and off she rushed, ready to share with the very first villager who happened to cross her path her newly gathered knowledge that I was certifiable. But the fact remains, weeds or no weeds, campions are dainty and beautiful, and if you take a minute to examine one of these pink flowers closely, you will discover a small detail that usually escapes the attention: in their very heart they sport a tiny delicate crown which is sometimes white, sometimes of the palest pink, and it is this little addition that contributes to their peculiar charm. However, as to the gnomes' responsibility for their presence in my garden, allow me once again to refrain from further comment. The thought merely amuses me, and it is nice to think that gnomes might have been responsible for my campions. As well as for one or two other very special surprises this spring.

The first one I discovered after a friend and I had discussed the nuisance of certain flying insects and how difficult it is to cope with them if one is against spraying (which I am, very much). Something must have overheard this conversation, for a few hours later I discovered a curious guest in the Gnome Garden: a small rosette of round, brownish red leaves, each leaf bordered with a tiny tiara of glistening diamonds. Though I had never seen this plant in my life, I recognized it immediately from my wildflower book: a round-leaved sundew, known for its intriguing habit of supplementing its diet by catching insects with those diamonds, which are nothing but a drop of glue. Once an insect becomes trapped, the leaves simply fold up and the plant starts its digestive procedure. True, the number of insects thus caught is extremely small, but then, gnomes are small too and probably think accordingly.

Another morning, not so long ago, I discovered an unusual blade of green pushing through the dark soil. It looked unfamiliar, and it was too young and too small to be identified. In any other garden it would have been pulled out there and then, but in mine, needless to say, it was left undisturbed.

It grew fast, and a week later its first leaves had assumed their definite form. I was thrilled, for I recognized it as a species of wild orchid. Which one exactly is hard to say. I'll have to wait until it produces flowers. But an orchid it is, and I have no doubt whatever that it will burst into bloom one of these days. And when that happens, I intend to give a special party for it. Yes, the gnomes will be invited too.

Splash!

As far back as I can remember I have had a vivid interest in water and all creatures living in it — in the magic of a glassy surface in which fragile reflections of reeds and trees and clouds mingle with a strange and silent underwater world. My very first memories are related to water, to the immense stretch of azure that dominated the view from our apartment in Monte Carlo. Whenever I looked out the window, it was there. When my mother took me down for our swim once a day, I could feel it and taste it. The deep blue sea never failed to puzzle me, because as soon as we plunged into its surf, it ceased to be blue. It became a crystal mystery. It caused the pebbles on its bottom to quiver strangely and it made my legs look funny and short. And most important of all, there was a coming and going of small fish and other tiny creatures that added to this underwater magic. They absolutely fascinated me, and I gave them my undivided attention. To be separated from them at the end of our swimming session was an ever-recurring dramatic event, and my wish to be forgotten and left sitting in the gentle waves was never granted. Even pretending to be a fish was of no use; somehow my mother always recognized me.

When I was older, we moved into a small village in an agricultural community, where my aquatic pursuits became somewhat more defined. Now we were surrounded by fields and meadows and pastures that were crisscrossed by innumerable little ditches and streams and brooks and other bodies of water. Their banks offered unlimited diversion, and for hours I could wander along the soggy watersides, armed with my fishing net and a jam jar. With infinite patience I scooped out numerous creatures, from which I selected the most interesting species to add to the collection of minnows and beetles and tadpoles that somehow survived in rows of jars on my windowsill.

Inevitably the years came when other quests of life had to prevail. As society began to claim my attention, my interest in all things aqueous dwindled. Or did it? I guess not. Always, when chancing upon water, be it lake, sea, river, pond, or pool, I find myself drawn to it. Ponds in particular, however small, possess a magnetism that I can seldom resist, and when I discovered a small and most unsightly pool of water in the garden of the cottage I was about to buy, it helped me in my final decision. True, the pond was depressingly diminutive and neglected, and its sides were overgrown with irises and forget-me-nots and ordinary grasses. But it met the basic requirements: there was water in it, which was so clear that I could see the bottom, and yes, even some swimming things! All it needed was a little remodeling and some clearing away of the too luxuriant aquatic growth. So plans were developed and lists were made. I had dreams of little fountains, maybe even a small, spouting dolphin.

When one sunny day in spring I finally found some time and courage to start this project, I noticed on the pond's narrow stone edge two common frogs, a tiny green frog, and a fat, insouciant toad. They were sitting close together and basking in the sun. I bent over to have a close look at them. Immediately the green frog jumped back into the pond. But the other two frogs and the toad were not in the least disturbed by my presence. Their little bodies, broad and relaxed in the enveloping warmth of the early May sun, remained motionless, and I could not find it in my heart to interrupt their precious moment of leisure; it would have been sheer cruelty. The next day they had taken up the same positions, and once again I left them in peace.

Weeks went by, and I did nothing to the pond. In the meantime the frog population increased. At times I would count as many as seven, all sitting peacefully together. Mr. Toad, too, usually joined in the fun. I completely abandoned all plans to "improve" the pond. Surely, if these riparians were so happy, it needed no further improvement? After all, it was *their* pond. For all I knew, they might have been living there for years (frogs and toads can live to a very old age), so who was I to disturb their peaceful life by destroying their home?

When I found out about my neighbor's ceaseless struggle to glorify his own pond (the one with the gnomes around it, remember?), I was even more convinced that I should leave mine untouched. From day one he experienced disaster. He did all kinds of gruesomely professional things to it in order to create a perfect environment for his plants and goldfish. He and his wife were always running about with peculiar equipment, calling mysterious messages to each other, like "The pee-aytch is much better today, dear!" (It was not until much later that I found out all there was to know about the importance of pH in a pond.) But whether it had been good that day, or any other day, I doubted very much, because things in their pond were continually dying at an alarming rate. Their entire goldfish population was wiped out in the course of a single week, and occasionally dead mice were found floating in it. To compensate for their losses I once presented them with a frog from my pond; it was back with me within three hours. (Frogs have individual markings that make identification very easy, and I know each of my frogs personally.)

But all their misery and suffering served at least one good cause: it convinced me that human intervention is not always beneficial, and it strengthened my belief that nature is often best left to follow her own course. I kept my pond in its original state, and I was never sorry I did. It became a home for countless uninvited but very welcome guests. It is now in its fifth year, and the three little goldfish that I put in the first year, to add a little color and to fight mosquito larvae, who are totally unwelcome, have grown into fat and large and lazy creatures, though I absolutely never feed them. (My neighbors, who meticulously feed their fish with well-balanced and exquisite melanges of nourishment, recently had to replace them all after yet another outburst of some mysterious malady.) Frogs and toads never fail to put in an appearance as soon as they emerge from their hibernal quarters. (In case you didn't know, frogs hibernate buried deep in the mud at the bottom of the pond, though they do not always sleep, for on several occasions I have seen them emerge and swim in circles under the ice.

Toads, in contrast, stay on the land and survive the rigors of winter by digging snug holes under logs, stones, and the like.)

This year my pond yielded a surprise: I discovered a hideous but intriguing life form, a miniature prehistoric monster that swam around or sat on the iris leaves just under the surface. My book revealed its identity: nymph of a dragonfly. One day in June I saw it leave its wet environment, climb up to well above water level, and settle on a leaf. A few hours later a breathtaking event took place before my very eyes: its back split open and out crawled an insect of imposing size and stunning beauty. A dragonfly! Its diaphanous wings very slowly unfolded and absorbed the rays of the sun. Then suddenly it started to vibrate, and up it flew into the clear summer sky, deliriously darting around in ever-widening circles.

It is not only the fauna that treats me to pleasant surprises. The yellow irises too are endowed with an unexpected peculiarity: they weep! Yes, they produce tears, as I found out quite accidentally one summer night. It was already dark, and I had just switched on the small Japanese lamp behind the pond, installed for the sole benefit of Mr. Toad, who is particularly active at nighttime and who thrives on the insects that are attracted by this illumination. As I watched him crawling about on his hunt for small game, I noticed a single tiny sparkle on the very tip of one of the iris leaves. What could it be? It was still too early for dew. I gently touched this liquid diamond, expecting perhaps some sticky matter that could be drawn into a thin transparent thread upon withdrawal of my finger. But no, at the slightest touch it fell off into the pond with a curiously melodious and limpid *drip!*

I sat down and watched. Slowly, very slowly, more jewels sprouted from the tips of other leaves, and soon hundreds of tiny teardrops twinkled in the light of the lamp. The drops grew bigger and bigger, and the tops of the leaves began to bend under their weight. Then, one by one, the diamonds fell back into the pond, *drip, drip, drip,* in a rich scale of musical notes, and the leaves, relieved of their burden, straightened up again.

Without doubt there is a scientific explanation for this phenomenon. In fact, a quick glance in my 1894 edition of *The Natural History of Plants* (which, in spite of its age, is one of the most complete works I have ever come across) revealed an entire chapter on the "Regulation of Transpiration" of leaves. I have decided not to read it, for the time being at least. I prefer to remain blissfully ignorant and maintain the illusion that my irises weep their very own tears. But since they have little reason for sadness in their undisturbed corner of the pond, I can but conclude that their tears are tears of joy.

Nocturnes

A GARDEN, most of us will agree, is very much a daytime affair. Not only is daylight one of the bare necessities for all things green and growing; we too need light to put our imaginations and green fingers to work, and ultimately to enjoy our floral riches. How we achieve this greatly depends on our natures and individual tastes.

I believe there are two species of gardeners, those who toil away the livelong day in a fury of digging, weeding, clipping, and pruning, for the mere sake of being engaged in physical gardening activities, and those who stoop to earthly labor so that later they may enjoy the results and wander in a haze of ecstasy along their sunlit borders, bending over each rose and deeply inhaling the ambrosial scent. I'm afraid I belong to the latter school, and I must confess that I include rather nondescript and useless activities in my routine, such as hours of reveling in lethargic laissez faire, hidden in the seclusion of my secret garden.

But whatever our horticultural pursuits, daylight is undeniably the vital link between us and our gardens. No one in a proper frame of mind will go weeding at midnight; after sunset even the most exuberantly flowering Dorothy Perkins sheds its dainty charms, and as darkness deepens it will be almost impossible to distinguish it from the lowly bramble bush.

As soon as the shadows are gathering, we retire. We have baths or showers to rid ourselves of the soil and sweat of the day's labor. Sometimes we sneak out again at night and sit on our patio or porch, with an electric light overhead, or maybe a candle on the table; but beyond that magic circle of light rises a wall of darkness, and the garden simply ceases to exist. Or does it?

I once knew a wonderful old lady. She owned a tiny thatched cottage surrounded by the smallest possible plot, which she had transformed into a miniature paradise, a garden so delicately designed that it reminded me of an exquisite piece of Queen Anne needlework. Gardening was her big passion in life, and although she had the odd man to help her out with the more tiresome chores, she did most of the work herself. I can still picture her kneeling on a small, threadbare cushion in front of her narrow borders, which contained an amazing variety of sweet-smelling flowers and herbs. She caressed the dark soil with her frail hands or tenderly stroked a single lavender bush or a soft, feathery tuft of fennel. You see, this lady was blind and she saw with her hands. Her sensitive fingertips recognized each stem, each flower, each leaf. With astonishing accuracy she registered growth and decay, and unwanted weeds had very little chance of survival. From numerous chats I learned a great deal from her. She opened my mind to unknown dimensions: the soft touch of a furry leaf, the fragrance of an unusual plant or flower, the intriguing sound of popping seedpods. Once she confided to me that the hours around midnight were her favorite moments for gardening, because only then, undistracted by the hubbub of civilization, could she fully enjoy the magic of sense, scent, and sound. She challenged me to try it, and I promised her I would.

"It does make sense," I said, "in the silence of the night . . ."

She cut me short. "Ah, silence," she said. "There is no such thing, dear."

I have never forgotten those words, for they are ultimately true. Silence does not exist. Silence is a patchwork of little sounds, but all too often we turn a deaf ear to it. Yet it surrounds us everywhere, most of all in our own gardens. And if you don't believe me, I'll show you. There is a way to find out.

It is almost midnight on a windless summer night. I invite you to sit down with me at the old cast-iron table in a remote corner of my garden, away from all the lights of the house. Wrap a throw around your knees to ward off the evening chill, for we'll sit here quite a while, and we'll hardly move. But I promise you a great experience: we are going to gather an unusual bouquet, an exquisite posy of sounds.

Let us start immediately with the most common vibration, for it can hardly escape our attention: the numerous insectile chirrings and chirpings and rustlings. Too numerous, in fact, to be individually discerned. The more we listen to them, the sleepier we'll get, for they blend into one monotonous, mesmerizing sound, which will hypnotize us if we're not careful. The trick is to accept it solely as a backdrop for what we are about to experience, and having done so, we shall henceforth ignore it for the sake of more important sounds.

Hush, don't speak. Do you hear that? It is deceptively like the hissing of a toy steam engine or a tiny train, but you are wrong to assume that there is a child at play at this hour. No, it is nothing less than a hedgehog, defending his territory against an intruder. He'll very likely pass by in a short while, and if you sit perfectly still, he might even sniff at your feet and gobble up that enormous slug that is about to crawl over your shoe. And what do you hear now, in the tree above us? Mice? Yes, it does sound somewhat like a nibbling mouse, but the sound is very feeble, and it would have to be a wee mouse indeed. It deceived me too the first time I heard it, but I assure you, there are no mice in my trees. What you hear is in fact a colony of wasps, about which I promise to tell you a thing or two in a later chapter. Not only are they active in the daytime, once at home they also indulge in mysterious nightly activities that produce this sound. They live in their large, perfectly round nest hanging under one of the branches, a well-concealed, miraculous piece of architecture. I would never have discovered it but for this gentle ticking noise, and since they live at a safe distance and have not shown any sign of aggression, I have allowed them to stay.

And now be prepared for a special treat. Immediately behind us is a patch of tall, wild pink balsam. The plants have been in bloom for some time, and already they bear a lot of ripe seedpods, which burst open at the slightest touch. All we need at this moment is someone or something to touch them — for instance, a big moth, of which there are many around, attracted by the scents of the night. There comes one now. You can't see it, of course, but you can hear its fluttering wings among the leaves.

Tickkk!! Did you hear that? What a charming, brittle

sound: one of the pods just opened. And immediately it was followed by another sound, difficult to describe, but let me give it a try: tiny raindrops bouncing on the leaves? Or perhaps an audience of applauding elves? I leave it to your imagination, as long as you don't forget that these pods are extremely powerful. They fling their bounty high and wide into the air, and the applauding elves are the seeds that land all around us.

And yes, you're right: that *was* a frog in my pond, just after the splash (which I'm afraid you may have missed) of a playful golden orfe in a nocturnal mood. My frogs are very well behaved and don't keep the entire neighborhood awake with nonstop croaking concertos as some frogs do, a habit to which, by the way, they owe their local nickname, "farmers' nightingales." What a whimsical name, so full of humor, of poetry.

Meanwhile it is practically impossible that you missed the voice of the very spirit of the night: an owl hooting, and another one answering. I have never understood why filmmakers always employ owls to enhance their creepy products. Vampires and werewolves invariably perform their bloody deeds accompanied by at least one owl hooting. It is not fair. I'm sure that owls are not at all charmed by these creatures of imagination; they are, at any rate, considerably less bloodthirsty.

I apologize for carrying on, for you just missed out on a very rare and special sound. I'm afraid your ear will have to learn how to catch it: the soft and gentle *thump-a-thump-a-thump* of a wood mouse crossing the lawn. Let me tell you this: when covering a long distance (and my lawn is, by wood-mouse standards, a very long distance indeed), they employ a unique method, hopping like kangaroos on their hind legs in long, graceful leaps.

It is getting late. Morpheus is calling us. But I hope that you begin to understand what this lady meant when she stated that there is no such thing as silence. We only experienced a few moments of it, but believe me, the silence of the night has many and various voices, and nowhere can they be heard better than in our own familiar surroundings. After sunset even the most common of nature's voices, the wind in the trees, assumes a touch of magic. The patter of the petals of a fading rose being shed on the terrace turns, for one fleeting moment, into an elfin ballet. You may even hear the rustling of feathers as a blackbird hen stirs in her sleep while sitting on her eggs. Or a dead leaf that dances a swishing pirouette in a sudden draft. If you allow yourself to spend a few nights in your garden, you will soon get acquainted with nature's orchestrations, with all their andantes and adagios. And eventually a new harmony will reveal itself to you: your garden's very own nocturnes.

Books Forever

NOT SO VERY LONG AGO my appetite for the newest books on the subjects of gardening and nature was unappeasable, and I would not be surprised if at some point my little gray cells may have turned green. Some peculiar and irresistible attraction invariably lured me into the gardening sections of bookshops, and no sooner had I picked up the latest glossy volume than my mind went blank. As I continued to leaf through page after page of sumptuous photography, reality ceased to exist and I was plunged into a deep horticultural trance. Not until I found myself out in the street again, blinking in the bright light of the afternoon and feeling the weight of these thoughtlessly purchased treasures cut into the flesh of my fingers, did I snap out of it. By then, however, it was too late. Several questions would arise almost immediately. How on earth was I going to find another foot of space on my shelves? Could even a single one of these new books at least show me how to transform my garden from its present condition of freelance chaos into a disciplined paradise? In other words, did I actually *need* any more books? The answer usually was "none of the above," and for the umpteenth time I would promise myself to be a trifle more selective on my next shopping spree, and exercise a little more self-control.

Meanwhile my bookcase was evidently beginning to show the strain of its increasing burden. The shelves were bending in an alarming way and had to be supported by even more books stacked between them. When one day I unsuccessfully tried to squeeze in a thirty-page brochure from our local nurseryman, the whole contraption collapsed altogether. The result was most startling: twenty-eight books sustained damage, with broken bindings or pages that had become dislodged, or both. A sad but revealing detail was that these were all new books, while my old volumes (some of which have been out of print for some 120 years) got through this catastrophe unscathed.

Tempting though it may be to ascribe this phenomenon to the powers of some protective bibliophilic fairy (and by now you most probably know that I'm a great subscriber to miracles and benevolent spirits), the only obvious explanation was, of course, the superior craftsmanship of the older books, and the use of materials that are, unfortunately, no longer available. Yet upon being confronted with this evidence of bibliopegistic shortcomings, I found the experience slightly traumatic, and I promised myself there and then that no new books, or at least no cheap editions, were to cross my threshold ever again, if I could help it.

So far I have kept my promise. I have developed a marked penchant for used gardening books, the older the better. I like their sturdy cloth or leather bindings. I enjoy their elaborate prose, so frequently marbled with snippets of poetry. I appreciate their typefaces, which often betray the use of those sturdy, old-fashioned printing machines that lasted for generations. I simply love the unexpected gifts that some books shed onto my desk, little spirits from the past, like clippings from old newspapers or magazines, pressed flowers and leaves that have become brittle with age, or even little insects that somehow got trapped and flattened between the pages. But above all I like the evidence of previous ownership: names and inscriptions on front pages and notes scribbled in the margins, the more the better.

Let me give you an example. Last year I chanced upon a book entitled *The Ideal Gardening Book, Illustrated.* Its very title harbored an enigma, and it was the word *ideal* that intrigued me. I couldn't quite work it out: was this an ideal book, or might it perhaps reveal ways to ideal gardening? A quick glance through its pages showed that it was by no means a classic of garden literature; rather, it was written and edited with muddled notions of order. Its introduction seamlessly passed into regular text, thereby unintentionally transforming the entire book into an oversized preface, and it was only vaguely divided into sections — one could hardly call them chapters — which bore no relation to each other. For instance, *The Wall Garden,* starting halfway down page 45, was followed by *The Violet* at the bottom of page 48. Most sections ended with some curiously flamboyant statement, like "Let us endeavor to leave our landmark on what was once our possession, so that in years to come we may be remembered with gratitude by the individual and the community," at the end of the section called *Trees and Shrubs.*

There were some other mysteries as well. The book's origin was utterly obscure. It revealed neither a publication date nor so much as a hint of any author or, in spite of some delightful illustrations, artist. Instead it contained a veritable treasure of less anonymous, handwritten information. "To Hums, from Willie, Christmas 1936" it said on the front page, and another old-fashioned handwriting on the endpaper reveals "30th Oct 1951. 4 new Mc. Gredy roses, right top bed" followed by "Bramley. Small tree. Transplanted '53. Very good, 30 apples!" It somehow created an immediate bond between Hums and me, if Hums it was who planted those roses and the apple tree. It couldn't have been Lucy Forrester from Bangor, N. Ireland, who became the owner of this book as late as 1956, according to an inscription on the second page. Or Karl Medlicott, who scribbled his name under those of Hums and Willie over three decades later: May 30, 1988. My name followed soon: I penciled it in even before I had paid for the book.

One of my most precious finds, however, is a small work about violets. It oozes nostalgia, and contrary to *The Ideal Gardening Book* it has everything one expects from a proper book: an author, an illustrator, and a date (January 1912). It also has twelve gnats and a small earwig flattened and preserved between the pages. These conjure up a charming vision: one of the previous owners ("J. P. Jackson, Her Book," it reads on the title page) wandering through her garden in the golden sweetness of an afternoon in May, clad in diaphanous lace. With this very same book in hand — and her umbrella in the other — she compares her own treasured violets with those in the wonderful color illustrations. Its most precious ingredient, however, is the "List of Violets," which is, if anything, bewildering. It contains names and descriptions of no fewer than fifty-five (fifty-five!) varieties. Among these I read, "BOSTON. Resembles Kaiser Wilhelm, same habit as Baroness the Rothschild," and I'm at a loss. This is too much, and I have a temporary vision of the mustachioed German monarch running around in baronial travesty. But isn't Blanche de Chevreuse (white, with rosy center) just too delightful a name, and wouldn't one spend one's very last penny in order to have a border full of them, only to be able to invite one's visitors into the garden and casually remark, "Do come and have a look at my Blanches de Chevreuse. They're *à point*"?

This little book also offers advice that is often both poetic and enigmatic, such as "But whatever the soil may be — clayey or sandy, or loamy — if diligent use be made of spade and hoe, the ground kept clean and sweet, fragrant flowers and healthy plants will recompense the cultivator's care." This revelation absolutely delighted me. I had to do my utmost to prevent myself from running out into the garden and scattering quantities of sugar over the borders with shouts of glee, for the book says the ground should be kept sweet, and lo, sweet it be!

Please forgive me. When on the subject of old gardening books, I lose all sense of restraint, and I tend to become frivolous and sentimental. Frivolous enough to conclude that perhaps it *was* a fairy, after all, who caused my shelves to collapse, in an effort to teach me an important lesson: that it is high time to invite some of our ancestors' values back into our gardens. And onto our bookshelves.

Consider the Trees

"FRIENDSHIP IS a sheltering tree," Samuel Taylor Coleridge, poet and philosopher, very touchingly observed 170 years ago. Throughout the ages poets have sung the praise of trees. It is perhaps significant that in our earliest literature the first two forms of vegetation ever mentioned by name are trees: the Tree of Life and the Tree of Knowledge, in the Book of Genesis. From that moment on, trees have continued to wave their branches into the life and language of thousands of generations. Civilizations ancient and new have worshiped trees and endowed them with mystic powers. On numerous occasions sad and joyous, trees have been planted as symbols of freedom. Trees have supplied the wood for our cradles; trees too will accompany us in death. Indeed, nature's greatest gift to mankind is the tree, and of this I'm firmly convinced: the bond between trees and us is of far greater importance than we shall ever realize.

In my life too, trees have played a more or less important part, and planting a tree was one of my first official deeds. I remember the occasion very well, for it was in the year that witnessed the great floods in my home country, the Netherlands, well over forty years ago, when thousands of people perished. I was only eleven years old and unable to grasp the full significance of this catastrophe, especially since my family did not suffer any losses. On the contrary, the whole affair rather annoyed me, for the grownups continually told me to shut up while they huddled around our Bakelite radio (we had no television in those days), trying to pick up the latest bulletins. Even the numerous graphic photos in newspapers and magazines failed to arouse emotions in me, with one exception: a soaked and lonely black-and-white cat, desperately clinging to life and to the branches of a treetop that barely stuck out above the fury of the water. My heart went out to this animal, and since I was unable to shed tears over the loss of human lives, I entered into the proper spirit by working myself into a frenzy of grief over the fate of this doomed creature. I strongly felt that something must be done for this cat, but alas, I could think of nothing. So I decided to imitate the adult world and opt for a symbolic deed: I would plant a tree in memory of the Unknown Cat.

Without revealing my motivation, I asked permission — and got it — to plant a tree near the garden gate. I found one in the neglected yard around our old village church. It was about three feet high, but since it had no foliage, I did not know what kind it was. Neither did I have the faintest idea how to treat it, and consequently I did all the wrong things. I simply pulled it out, shook the soil from its torn and damaged roots, and planted it in the hole that I had already dug. It should on all accounts have withered away and died within months, if not weeks. But it didn't. As time advanced it even developed a few leaves and manifested itself as a birch. But it didn't noticeably grow. In fact, careful measuring revealed that I grew faster that first year, a discovery that gave reason for some concern. Trees grow to greater heights than people, I knew, but since I was now outgrowing a tree, I concluded that I was destined to become a giant. I foresaw problems: soon I would be too big even for my own room, and a special building might have to be constructed to house me. This minor inconvenience, however, would be greatly compensated for by the power and great strength that my gargantuan dimensions would doubtlessly bring about, not to mention my schoolmates' envy.

But the following year my fears proved unwarranted:

the tree gained about ten inches in a single season, and two years later I began to look up at it. By the time we moved out of town it had reached a height of about seven feet, and in its silvery trunk it had developed a peculiar twist. It was without much feeling, however, that I said goodbye to it. I had reached an age at which other pursuits began to prevail. It was, after all, only a tree, and I didn't really care that I would never see it again. Or did I?

The truth is, I never entirely forgot this particular tree. At times its ghost would pop up, but never for more than a fleeting moment. I would wonder what might have become of it. Cut down, more than likely. And after such thoughts the ghost would be insulted, and sulk, and rapidly vanish again.

Two summers ago, while touring around the country, I suddenly found myself in the neighborhood of my old home. In all those years I had never been back, and inevitably the image of my tree popped up again in all its seven-foot-glory, twist in trunk and all. It tugged at my sleeve, so to speak, begging me to come, if only for old times' sake. At the same time I feared the worst; in forty years this once rural area had been urbanized and had changed almost beyond recognition. It was unlikely that the tree, or even the old house, had escaped the ravages of our ever-advancing civilization. But when I discovered the familiar spire of the church above the strange new developments, the powers of sentiment became too much to resist.

The house was still there, and I recognized my tree almost immediately by its funny twist. But it was no longer my seven-foot silver birch. It had grown into a breathtaking giant that rose majestically above the low house and hung far over the gate. I parked the car further along the street, got out, and walked slowly toward the old gate. This was a dream; no, this was sheer magic. It was all still there: the house, so much smaller now, the squeaky wrought-iron garden gate, and *my* tree! I looked up into its canopy, a myriad of pale green leaves that quivered in the golden light of the afternoon. There were birds in it, and at its very top I discovered a nest, probably belonging to a family of magpies but now deserted. Then I noticed the sidewalk immediately under the tree: it was carpeted with a thick layer of fine brown seeds that the tree was shedding in dense clouds each time the wind breathed through its branches.

An idea occurred to me. I bent down, collected a handful of seeds, and stuffed them in my pocket. These I would take home. I would prepare a patch of soil in my Gnome Garden and scatter the seeds over it. If they came up and grew, I would select the healthiest specimen and give it the best possible care.

I now have twenty-eight seedlings in my garden, little baby birches, and I have selected the strongest one destined to live on. It is barely a foot tall, but already its two tiny branches are struggling to reach the sky. I hope I'll live to see the day when it will tower high above me. When I'll be able to rest in its shadow. And when, in my dotage, it will offer me its sheltering friendship.

More Trees

I think that I shall never see
A poem lovely as a tree . . .
Poems are made by fools like me,
But only God can make a tree.

WHATEVER MIGHT HAVE inspired the American poet Joyce Kilmer to write his frequently quoted poem "Trees" in 1913, it certainly reflects his esteem for the ruler of the plant kingdom. If only we would all share his view, our globe would be a very different place. Our need and greed, however, take the upper hand, and worldwide our forests are rapidly dwindling. What took millions and millions of years to evolve will be wiped out in a few generations if we're not careful.

True, we are gradually becoming aware of this problem, and yes, I may sound like a parrot, simply repeating what we hear all the time. Newspapers and magazines confront us with the sad state of our woods almost daily. Television too pours it over our breakfast tables, so to speak. Omniscient savants spurt their warnings with the monotonous regularity of a geyser. Or, if we're truly "lucky," we may even see this devastation happen before our own eyes, in our own neighborhoods.

We, you and I, are all part of the global conspiracy against our arboreal allies. I certainly am, in more ways than one. The luxurious log fire in my hearth right now, comforting though it may be, serves an ornamental purpose only. And if only you could see the table at which I'm writing these very words: its solid, wide top is made from a single shelf that must have come from a tree at least 200 years old. The table itself is about 150 years old, but if it hadn't been for this piece of furniture, and a motley variety of nephews and nieces in the form of cabinets and consoles and maybe even a pulpit or two, this tree might still have been alive and thriving. It might have been a home for birds and beasts, and under its crown lovers might have found shelter and shade. Now it is sentenced to support my word processor; one can hardly imagine a more mundane task.

But really, I'm not such a bad guy, in spite of these confessions. On the contrary, I'm probably too tolerant when it comes to trees, for after I pulled out approximately 150 uninvited baby oak trees, I discovered that I *still* have a stunning 85 trees left in my tiny garden. I hasten to add that so far the vast majority of them barely reach my shoulder. The smallest one, the tiny silver birch of exceptional parentage, is only a foot tall, but nevertheless a tree it is.

For the sake of trees I even break laws occasionally: I smuggle them into the country, an act upon which the agricultural powers that be will most definitely frown. My mountain ash, for instance, is such an illegal migrant; it miraculously survived three days in a suitcase and thousands of miles of air travel.

It all started in Sitka-by-the-Sea, Alaska, where I once spent an entire summer. I had seen, and ignored, mountain ashes before, and in retrospect I wonder how I could possibly have failed to recognize their magic. But the moment that I met my first mountain ashes in Alaska, I fell hopelessly in love with them. It was as though they were all clamoring for my attention. They did their utmost to impress me with their dark and sturdy trunks, encrusted with bright patches of stunning turquoise lichens. They serenaded me with their full crowns festooned with dollops of snowy blossoms that wafted their heavy scent as far as the wind could carry it. And as the season advanced, they cast a spell on me with their dense clusters of berries, which continually changed color, from green to the palest orange to almost scarlet, with every possible nuance in between.

When, in late September, it was time to go, I had reached the conclusion that life without a mountain ash was not worth living. I simply had to get hold of one, even if I had to resort to illicit methods. So prior to my departure, at the crack of dawn, I sneaked to the very edge of the village and dug up a perfect seedling specimen of about fifteen inches. Back in my hotel room, I wrapped it in plastic and hotel towels (which I sent back with a word of apology) and cleverly concealed it in one of my suitcases. It occupied so much room that I had to dispose of a pair of boots and several items of almost brand-new clothing. I'll never forget the somewhat startled look the lady of the Salvation Army gave me when I deposited these garments on her counter; she was obviously not used to such glamorous bestowals.

When I finally arrived home (and yes, I *did* manage to fool the powers that be, who never even took a peep into my suitcases), I was practically collapsing with fatigue. Yet I immediately proceeded to plant my new addition in a large Italian terracotta urn. In those days, you see, I had no garden yet — just a sixth-floor patio where all things green and growing lived strictly in a weird medley of pots and urns and containers. But when I had finished the job and stood back to admire it, I had to admit that my poor sapling looked disheveled and slightly ridiculous. It dawned on me that in my ignorance I had perhaps been a little too enthusiastic and impulsive, for it was inconceivable that this pathetic little tree could ever grow into a pillar that might one day support the sky. Rather would it pine away, and wither, and eventually die.

It did no such thing, and in the spring that followed its height increased by at least another foot. Then, in late summer of that same year, I moved into my cottage. The little mountain ash moved with me. It was in fact the very first thing I planted in my garden, and it promptly lost all its leaves in the process, long before the other trees started to shed their foliage. Yet its bare twigs retained their flexibility, a sure sign that it was not giving up and that it still held the sap of life. When the days lengthened again and the first golden rays of springtime sun awoke all things dormant, the little tree happily joined in nature's seasonal festival by donning an attire of nine feathery leaves.

Now, five years later, it has reached a height of about eight feet, and last year it behaved extremely well by producing three small clusters of blossoms. These in turn soon developed into berries, which slowly ripened from pale to darker orange. But before they had a chance to turn red, the blackbirds discovered them. They feasted on them with whoops of delight, and three days later there was not a single berry left.

Meanwhile it became obvious that I had planted the tree too close to the only "big" tree in my garden, a twenty-five-foot aggressive oak with a trunk of about one foot in diameter. The oak was in its prime and showed no intention of slowing down in favor of its puny neighbor. It had to be taught a lesson. Better still, it had to go.

And it went. It now sits at the side of the house, neatly cut up in logs that in due time will be consigned to the flames of my fireplace. Which only proves that I'm no better than the rest of humanity after all. We all are constantly racing down the path of destruction, merrily nibbling away at our oldest and most precious of living organisms. We are in fact nothing but human termites. How much longer before an exterminator will decide to destroy us too?

The King Is Dead!

THERE WAS NO DOUBT about it, he had to go. He had become too feeble and too brittle. Too dangerous as well. After he had reigned ten times forty years, his hour had inevitably struck.

No, I'm not hinting at some unknown kingdom ruled by a demented monarch. I'm referring to the oldest resident of our area's main town. Yet in his own right he was certainly a monarch, considering a span of an amazing ninety feet from tip to tip of his extending branches. Yes, indeed, a tree, another tree. A linden, to be more specific. *Tilia vulgaris* is its official name, though at the dawn of its existence it might well have had another one, or none at all.

Its age remains a mystery. For generations it was believed to be at least eight hundred, if not a thousand years old, but recently an arborist declared it to be closer to four centuries in age. Certain it is, however, that its existence was recorded for the first time in the year 1662, when a globetrotter from France, the Count de Moncony, described it in his diary. Already in those days he was impressed by its dimensions: it took him over sixty paces to walk around the circumference of its majestic crown, and no less than twenty-seven pillars supported its outstretching branches. This is indeed a valuable description, for not only does it indicate that three centuries ago the tree had already reached a formidable age, it tells us too that from its infancy it had enjoyed a good deal of attention and proficient care.

From that year on it never failed to leave a trail of written records in the books, illustrating its importance in the daily doings of the citizens. Under its branches the township made official tidings known, and it became the designated place for marriage announcements. It knew considerably less romantic moments too, for in its greenish shade justice was administered and many sentences were carried out, including a beheading.

As its trunk began to lose the smoothness of its youth and developed strange and gnarly twists, it gave birth to tales and sagas. One of these myths, a legend of the Virgin, has survived until this very day. This is the story: Once upon a time there was a certain Anthony, who deviated from the path of virtue until one day he vanished altogether. It was assumed that he had lost his life on one of his marauding expeditions. But his pious mother could not believe this. She never lost her hope of seeing him again, and as a token of her faith she placed a statue of the Virgin Mary in the old tree's branches. There it stayed for many years, and slowly it decayed, until one day it was no more. But lo! One night another statue suddenly emerged from countless knots and nodules in the trunk. It was a miracle, if ever there was one! It seemed to smile and radiate with joy. And on that very day the lost son reappeared and showed remorse.

Here this simple legend ceases. It may have been a legend only, yet until recent times a mother and her child were clearly silhouetted in the trunk. On sunny winter days, when the low, pale light could freely play through leafless branches and cast fantastic shadows on the twisted bole, the likeness of these figures was wondrously enhanced, almost as if human hands had carved it out. But in the early sixties of our era the tree began to show signs of decline, through circumstances that I shall describe. It needed surgery, and in due time the effigy was totally erased.

But long before this sad event took place, council after city council continued to spend time and money on the tree. Halfway through the nineteenth century it was pruned and trimmed and trained into a giant Chinese canopy. It offered shelter, like a huge umbrella, against rain and shine. During unexpected summer storms it was a refuge for countless passersby, until the drip of rain at last began to penetrate the heavy foliage, but by then the storm had usually blown over and the sun had once again appeared.

It was a meeting point for young and old. They occupied the wooden benches to exchange their gossip and discuss the latest politics. During springtime evenings the heavy fragrance of its million blossoms wafted down and intoxicated lovers, inspiring them to whisper "Yes, I will" into one another's ears.

Then came the youngest century, as speedy and as hasty as no other century has ever been. Though the elderly still gathered for a chat and the young made love, they rarely did so under the tree, where the noise of rapidly increasing traffic drowned the human voice. Some of the benches had remained, and people still sat on them, but not for very long; life's rapids had become too fast, and there was no more time for leisure.

Traffic too began to claim its territory at the tree's expense. Concrete replaced the fertile soil, cutting off the elements of life, and gradually the tree was choked to death. Decay set in, and branch by branch it pined away.

The town did not give up yet. Tree experts were called in, and for years the tree had its own arborists, who carefully removed all rotting wood and did whatever they could do to stimulate new growth. But however hard they tried, their efforts were to no avail. Decay spread more and more and hollowed out its massive trunk. The few tall branches that were left had only minimal support. One day a branch snapped off and almost killed a toddler in the process, an incident that sealed its fate. The tree must go!

And so it went. But centuries of unremitting care from humans seemed to have endowed it with a sense of drama. It seemed to have anticipated its demise and did not go before a final show, an eighteen-karat miracle that left the township speechless.

The day and hour of the tree's removal were made known through our local press; by ten A.M. a large and silent crowd had flocked together to witness the event, which later was described as a dolorous farewell. A strategy had been worked out. A crane of sixty tons would be employed. The heavy branches were the first to be removed, after which the trunk would be cut through and lifted up onto a truck.

All went according to this plan. Meanwhile the "oldest citizen" was honored with a requiem: church bells tolled, and when the racket of the saws had ceased, the local choir sang a last adieu. The crowd was taciturn. From time to time some of the older ones produced a handkerchief and blinked a tear away. Finally the crane began its task, and slowly, very slowly, the trunk was hoisted up into the air.

And then a miracle occurred. As the hollow trunk was lifted from its ground, out popped two feeble branches. They fanned out like flowers in a posy, relieved after the removal of their confining paper. They had leaves too, though no more than perhaps one hundred. And there, in full view of the flabbergasted masses, stood a tiny trembling tree. It looked extremely shy and vulnerable, but without doubt a tree it was, a healthy one into the bargain. It had sprouted in the hollow womb of the decaying trunk, oblivious of any other world. It may have been a shoot from the old root that had obtained an independence of its own. It may have been a seedling that had germinated and survived for years by feeding on the rotting wood of its declining parent. Whatever was the case, it didn't matter in the least. It did not detract an iota from the significance of that astounding moment: on his deathbed the old monarch had appointed his successor, as a monarch should.

The king is dead, long live the king!

It is hard to fathom the emotions of all those hundreds witnessing this miracle. But unanimous was their reaction. After moments of dumbfounded silence, a murmur of amazement arose from the perplexed spectators. Bewilderment was evident on every face: could this be true, or was this perhaps a dream? But soon the audience began to cheer and chant: "Let it stay! Let it stay! Let it stay!"

It would be rewarding at this point to write that the old tree had triumphed, that the young sapling was allowed to stay and grow into another giant that might live to witness our future in the next millennium. But did it stay?

Oh, yes. For two more days. And then it was declared nonviable on its disturbed location, a verdict influenced more by already planned parking facilities than by reality, I fear. Nevertheless, the town's administrators took great care to show their readiness to save it. It was carefully dug out and, escorted by a motorcade, transported to a nursery. But there, uprooted from its mother soil, it clearly suffered from its trauma and showed no further interest in life. It never did survive.

Finicky Feeders

WINTER HAS COME once again, with its bleak, low light and long shadows. A first spell of frost has shot needle-fine crystal arrows across the dark surface of the silent pond, and many wild creatures draw closer to the house. I do not want to disappoint them, and now, during these dark days of the year, I have many additional beaks to feed. From dawn to dusk the garden is alive with the fluttering and chirping of countless winged eaters. Unfortunately, my efforts to compose well-balanced diets for a multitude of little stomachs are not always appreciated. I never cease to be amazed at the complexity and diversity of their tastes, and the abundant variety of birdfood offered on the pet shelves of our local supermarket do not make it any easier.

To this day I have not been able to find an ideal combination of prepacked nourishment to please all of my feathered friends. For instance, I discovered that a certain brand of birdfood, marketed as Seeds for Small Songbirds, attracted everything but songbirds. The singers pecked at it occasionally, uttered some disapproving squeaks (which probably meant "Yucch!"), and flew to the next dish on their menu. Then came the omnivorous magpie, who had a liking only for certain components of the mixture; for these he dug furiously, scattering most of the rest on the ground. These leftovers in turn enticed less welcome dinner guests: mice! They picked out the choicest grains and carried them off to their dens between the walls of the house, where they proceeded to behave like true party animals and challenged my nerves, especially after midnight. But bird and beast alike rejected the majority of these seeds altogether, as I found out in early spring, when a jungle of sinister grasses and bizarre weeds cropped up in the immediate vicinity of the feeding table.

It was the same all over with Pigeon Mix. I have a fondness for wild wood pigeons and turtle doves, whose soft, melancholic cooing ranks among the top ten of Mother Nature's soothing sounds. I had hoped to attract them with a specially selected delicacy. My efforts were, needless to say, in vain. The pigeons continued to devour quantities of stale bread that I put out for "general purpose," after which they would fly away and give cozy cooing concerti elsewhere in the neighborhood. The Pigeon Mix was favored mainly by the red squirrels, who in turn ignored a choice Squirrels' Melange. The blackbirds, however, discovered that the latter contained some fascinating ingredients, and they would stand knee-deep in it, picking out odd-shaped brown morsels that looked like some kind of dehydrated cat food.

I tried other ready-packed and higher-priced mixtures, but the scenario hardly changed. On the contrary, it was distressing to discover that prices usually were in inverted ratio to quality, and invariably each spring an uncanny quantity of weeds betrayed that such assortments contained a medley of useless materials (although one year I harvested a nice little crop of tiny, tasty carrots from between the tiles of the patio).

There are exceptions, of course. Old-fashioned suet balls never fail to attract crowds of quarreling titmice, but the speed at which these are consumed is quite exceptional, and halfway through a cold spell stores are usually sold out. They are not exactly cheap either, and besides, I found that they frequently spread a peculiar rancid odor as soon as they are brought indoors.

My obvious conclusion is that some producers of birdfood are rather more interested in our wallets than they are in birds. Moreover, I have a sneaking suspicion that they conspire with manufacturers of feeding stations, who deluge the market with all kinds of strange contraptions, including miniature cottages with low, thatched roofs and sometimes even chimneys. I too once fell for one of these charming but idiotic contrivances. But after a season of observing my feathered wildlife, I came to the firm conclusion that such feeding houses should be outlawed. Birds are, above all, creatures of the open air. They abhor having to go into any kind of confined space to obtain their food, and from a bird's point of view such constructions, though the sides may be open, are very confining indeed. A roof so low above their heads completely obscures their view of the immediate surroundings, where forever the Enemy May Lurk. (We should never forget that many creatures of the wild are particularly vulnerable when feeding.)

Certain other birdfeeders too should fall under the Cruelty Against Birds Act, and if such an act does not yet exist, it should be promulgated as soon as possible. I'm referring to those clear plastic containers in which we can conveniently observe how much is left. The birds see this too, of course. But unfortunately, they are unaware of the clear plastic, and I'm sure they must suffer a great deal of frustration and "beak shock" before they finally discover where exactly in this invisible barrier they can find access to their breakfast or lunch or dinner.

I could go on and on, for sadly enough, there are many such examples. The long and the short of it is that bird business is perhaps concentrated too much on pleasing the human eye, rather than on creating functional, bird-friendly products.

So one day I decided to render myself independent of pet-shop supplies. This was easy. First I built my own spacious feeding tables (two: one open and one with a simple roof high above it). Then, using only common supermarket ingredients, I invented my own winter birdfood recipes (I *never* feed my birds in summertime!). Of these, my most successful have been crunchy suet balls, and if you're interested in trying your hand at making some, this is what you need: good-quality suet or other fat (I don't believe in cheap stuff because it is "only for the birds"), shelled *unsalted* peanuts, sunflower seeds, pine nuts (nowadays readily available as an important ingredient for the fashionable Italian pesto sauce), raisins, chopped dried apricots, chopped dried apples, and a pair of plastic or rubber gloves to tackle a messy job. If you know of any other seeds or ingredients that might delight your winged locals, by all means use these too. But let me emphasize: beware of salt, a no-no for birds! Soften the fat over low heat in an old pan; it should not become too liquid, or too hot to handle. Mix in liberal — very liberal — quantities of the other ingredients, let everything cool somewhat, and form balls about the size of a tennis ball. Let these cool some more, then wrap and tie them in old, fine netting (I use plastic nets in which supermarkets frequently sell onions, garlic, and so forth). *Et voilà,* a scrumptious ball that will delight the palates of your feathered fauna. Serving suggestions: decorate an outdoor Christmas tree with these balls, and they will attract a flock of living ornaments. Or better still, hang one on the clapper of a wind chime and enjoy your grits or hash browns or cereal with a live morning symphony performed by breakfasting beaks.

Bon appétit!

Green Rooms

"Is there any difference between a house and a garden?"

If anyone had asked me this question six years ago, when life still whirled about in an endless urban maelstrom, I would probably have shrugged. I would have cast furtive glances over my shoulder to see if help was nearby, just in case. And of course my reply would have been politely affirmative, if not a trifle frigid. Then, after mumbling some excuse about having to catch a train, I would have hurried on. Trains, I found, were extremely handy when trying to rid oneself of company asking idiotic questions. But now, years later, the situation has vastly changed. I left the city and moved into a corner of civilization where no train can be a possible pretext.

Where the fastest movement caught by the eye is the swift flight of the swallows. And where my own life has slowed down to a pace hardly faster than that of a geriatric slug. Also, I have learned to think about questions asked and to take them a little more seriously. Allow me, therefore, to return to the initial question: is there any difference between a house and a garden?

There is but one correct answer: no. There is no difference whatsoever. Any house, but my house in particular, is as much a garden as a garden is a house, and as the years advance I find that the borderline between the two becomes increasingly vague. For some visitors, insects in particular, there is no borderline at all. My house has rooms, and so has my garden, and to the adventurous spider there is no difference between the beams of the ceiling and the bows of the chestnut tree. It feels equally at home on both. And so do I, although I prefer to sit *under* the tree rather than in it. Indeed, at this time of the year one corner of the garden has become my study. Here, at this very moment, I merrily type away on the keyboard of my word processor, for the day is glorious, and the butterflies are plentiful, and I see no possible reason that I should avoid the company of beast and bird and bug on behalf of work. On the contrary, there is something positively inspiring about the fact that a small ladybug just landed on the Q key and now merrily marches along the QWERTY path. Later today, when work is done, another corner in my garden will become the outdoor dining room, and I hope the flies and gnats won't decide to partake of our wine, though to drown in such sweet beverage must be infinitely less irksome than to suffocate in a waft of vicious insecticide.

Forgive me, I'm straying. An outdoor study may be inspiring, but by the same token the distractions are abundant. Especially when the chickadees repeatedly drop nesting material into one's coffee. As I said, my house is my garden, and vice versa, though to the cynical mind this statement may present some puzzles.

"But what about plants? You don't grow things indoors!" I can hear him gasp. I patiently and politely point out that there are two large ferns on the table, a positive Easter parade of begonias in the window, a deliriously exotic orchid on the sideboard (a present, needless to say), and, oh yes, a bunch of withering ivy cuttings in a jam jar on one of the bookshelves. (I'll wisely omit to mention a collection of seeds. These can be found everywhere — in tea tins, envelopes, an old sewing box, coffee mugs, cookie jars, and desk drawers. In my house nothing remains empty for very long.)

"But I mean *real* plants. And trees. And shrubs!"

I begin to lose patience. Is this poor cynic really blind? Can't he see that the table is like a tree? And that the chairs are rhododendrons and azaleas? Do I understand that he lacks even a *soupçon* of imagination to notice that furniture is to the inside of these walls what plants and trees and shrubs are to the outside? I try to point this out, but the cynic obviously reaches the conclusion that I'm a lost case. He states that he has a train to catch and beats a hasty retreat. Never to be seen again, I hope. I have no time for cynics.

Meanwhile, the more I think of it, the more I enjoy the comparison of furniture and vegetation. The idea of sitting in the easy rhododendron by the fire while November howls into the chimney is positively pleasing, and lazing in the shade of the armoire on a merry morning in May is too Elysian an experience to miss.

I must now hasten to admit that I do perceive some minor differences between my indoor and outdoor furniture, lest you too think I'm non compos mentis. One of the main characteristics of indoor furniture is that it hardly grows. Which in a way is regrettable, for it might lead to some entertaining conversation. Picture the following scene:

Enter a visitor. The moment she crosses the threshold, she claps her hand over her mouth in sheer admiration.

"Oh my dear, that table!" she gasps. "I don't recognize it. Why, it almost comes to my waist. What on earth did you feed it?"

"Nothing very special," I casually remark. "Just the regular thing, and maybe a hint of leg-improver once a week."

Whereupon my visitor turns around and notices the chair. She exclaims in tones of ecstasy, "And that chair! It is too wonderful! It was only minuscule when I last saw it. Oh please, do let me sit down in it . . . But tell me, where *are* you going to put it if it grows any bigger?"

To which the obvious reply is that it would have to go altogether. On second thought, perhaps it is just as well that furniture does not grow . . .

But fortunately, my outdoor furniture grows all the better. The newly planted walls of ivy and conifers around the tiny secret garden have grown quite dense during the past three years, and already they lend a promise of secrecy and mystery to what lies within them. (What lies within? Silence. Shelter. Serene solitude. No words can describe the joy of hiding in the green tranquillity of this secret room and pretending not to be at home.) Then there is my *armoire Provençal,* to which I referred earlier. This is my favorite rhododendron bush, which was still a baby when I planted it. It has now attained a respectable size, and if I squint at it from a horizontal position on my back in the grass, it does indeed vaguely resemble a French cupboard, provided I have had enough champagne.

I am not the only one to regard the garden as an extension of the house, for a sudden breeze bears on it the unmistakable smell of some aggressive detergent. It comes from across the lane, where the lady of the house is presently cleaning her garden path in a frantic effort to remove all signs of life. She is forever "cleaning" her garden, as indeed she refers to it (I've never heard her use the verb *to garden*). She literally vacuum cleans the lawn twice a week, and I have a sneaking suspicion that she very much regrets the nonexistence of a special grass shampoo. She does her borders too; these consist mainly of vast stretches of amazingly black earth, with here and there a tuft of green, scrupulously trimmed beyond recognition. And when finally the last speck of uninvited growth has been deracinated, she retires indoors and starts all over again. To her, there is no difference at all between her garden and her house, judging from the way she fervently employs identical cleaning methods for them.

But that's not entirely what I mean. What I meant to make clear is that my garden has become an integral part of my home, and I find it very hard to tell which is more important. True, the shelter of a roof above one's head is one of the essentials in life, but I would be lost without the feel of a living green carpet under my feet and the sight of three-dimensional paintings of lilies and laburnums, for these are the things that give me the reassuring sensation of being at one with life. And tell me, what is more essential in life than life itself?

Something Bugging You?

I'M NEVER ALONE in the garden. It is impossible to enjoy even a single minute of privacy. No matter whether I'm at work or reveling in a moment of leisure, I know that I'm surrounded by wary eyes. Take the robin, for instance. He is always lurking in the neighborhood, keeping an eye on me and ready to swoop down at the first sign of activity. The very sound of a squeaking shed door is enough to entice him from whatever business he is conducting, for well he knows this squeak, which usually announces some form of horticultural occupation: a session of hoeing, for instance, or, even better, digging. Every robin knows that digging is serious business, for with any luck it will yield a rich harvest of worms and larvae and grubs and other scrumptious vermicules that are normally beyond beak reach.

All this, however, is by the way, as it is not my intention to elaborate on the robin's doings. Although I very much enjoy the antics of this little red-breasted harlequin, I was really referring to the lesser forms of life when I stated that one is never alone. Anything with *more* than four legs, in fact, or none at all. In other words, let's now indulge in a session of critter-watching.

In the garden every square foot is teeming with life. Or rather, every cubic foot, for life is a three-dimensional affair that cannot be expressed in simple surface measurements. From the deepest garden soil to the highest treetops, you will hardly come upon a single stretch of space that is not occupied by some creature or another. So let us start with the basics, the earth under our feet, and let us submit to the robin's wish and do some digging. The moment we stab our spade deep into the soil and wiggle it about, out crawls our first encounter: a worm. True, it is hardly the elevated sort of company with whom we are dying to engage in entertaining conversation, but that's not the point. The point is, we are not alone; we have been joined by another living organism (though not for very long, the robin will see to that), *quod erat demonstrandum.* If the worm has been particularly unfortunate, we may even have the company of two. A distressing experience, by the way, for I do not cherish cutting worms in half. Somehow I have never been convinced that it does not matter and that each half will continue to grow into a new specimen. Neither do I believe that the worm enjoys it. It will not squiggle in gratitude at our feet and say, "Thank you, oh Big Digger, for giving me a playmate!"

Don't misunderstand me, though; I do not, as a rule, maintain close relationships with worms. So at this point I shall leave the robin to deal with the victim, and I shall continue to focus on other members of my garden's population, for there are many more invertebrates, good, bad, and ugly, that require our attention. Let me start with some of the "bad" ones first, though I prefer to think that in the animal world there is no such thing as bad, in the human sense of the word. Insects can't help being pests, and they definitely don't enjoy being so. They are what they are, programmed to fulfill their mission: to survive and multiply. Unfortunately, their way of achieving this frequently interferes with our own plans. Take the ants, for instance, which, given the opportunity, will ruin one's lawn by turning it into a moon landscape. And not only that, they will also follow mysterious, meandering paths. They will find the tiniest cracks in walls or doors or windows. Next they will proceed indoors, and with astounding infallibility they will establish the precise location of one's sugar bowl and other containers with sweet sustenance. Therefore we have no alternative but to destroy them — eye for an eye.

Indeed, the destruction of ants is one of the activities in which I frequently indulge. All summer long I go about with kettles of hot water, which I pour over their nests (in the garden), or with cans of aggressive poison, which I spray or sprinkle on their paths (indoors). It is not something I enjoy doing, and, believe me or not, I always apologize to the ants first. I tell them how sorry I am, but really, they owe it to themselves. It is, of course, a war I never win, for which in a way I'm grateful. I would hate to have it on my conscience to have eradicated the entire ant population. Besides, I shall never forget the pleasure I derived when I was a boy from keeping ants in an artificially constructed nest; observing their mysterious doings whenever I lifted the lid off their glass-covered tunnels — which I had shaped out of clay — taught me more about the complex ways of society than years of tedious history lessons.

So let us give the ants no more thought and cast our eyes elsewhere. From the "bad" to the "ugly." What do we have, right here at eye level? I shiver, for here I see some really ugly company: an enormous spider. It has woven its intricate web between the branches of the magnolia tree. I'm sure it sees me too, but since I do not represent a tasty first course, it completely ignores me. I know perfectly well that it will do me no harm whatsoever. On the contrary, it will assist me in my continuous struggle against the "bad," but nevertheless it gives me the creeps. Which only goes to prove that in some ways this spider is superior to me, because it does not harbor ill or irrational feelings.

My arachnid discourse brings to mind a conversation I had with my nurseryman the other day. Or rather, his monologue, since my contribution was merely an occasional affirmative mumble. He is a great one for monologues, during which he liberally spouts his fountains of knowledge. It is not the kind of knowledge obtained from books. No. I strongly feel that he has acquired his wisdom from a much more trustworthy source, that is, many years of observation and experience, and he enjoys sharing it, laced with wisps of smoke from his pipe, with an interested soul. I'm a fervent nonsmoker, but I don't mind his pipe. In fact I like it. Out in the open it does not bother me in the least, and somehow it adds authority to his statements. It introduces an atmosphere of trust. If he would proclaim, in tones of utmost sincerity, that "spiders are . . . puff puff . . . in fact, related to . . . puff puff . . . the American eagle," I would not doubt his statement for one moment (whereas a cigarette dangling from the corner of his mouth would greatly distract from the credibility of this same statement). Yes, he is a great man. But unfortunately, his bills are great as well.

However, all that is neither here nor there. So let us return to his latest monologue, and to the ugly spider. This is what he stated on pests: "If it wouldn't be for spahders, we'd be wading knee-deep through insecks." Somehow I would believe him even if he didn't have that pipe.

Some insects, though, are too big for spiders, no matter how strong their webs. Take a dragonfly, for instance (one of the few insects that is both beautiful and ugly), which is sometimes bigger than a mouse. An intriguing creature if ever there was one, and most entertaining company. I marvel at its grace while it flits to and fro through the entire garden, a flash of brilliant blue, catching dinner (flies, mosquitoes) in its flight. It seems to know its territory very well, and when it takes a moment's rest to bask in the sun, it always chooses the same location: the very top of a single twig that protrudes above the hedge, or a certain section of the clothesline. It never remains there for long, though. Now it jumps up and hovers around in ecstatic circles, now it settles again on its favorite perch in the sun, proudly displaying its gold-powdered, transparent wings. It reminds me of an excited little girl in her favorite finery, unable to sit still at the prospect of an outing to a children's party. It also reminds me of a fairy tale, because I cannot think of any other creature with wings of such enchanting elfin qualities.

Bugs. They are always around us, day and night. No matter where we look, in every corner we see something crawling, trembling, fluttering, hovering. There is the colorful parade of butterflies, for instance. It is wonderful to follow them in their pursuit of nectar, rarely visiting the same flower twice — to watch their skittish games, their graceful aerial dances, or their frenzy when defending their plot against intruders, for some species have an amazing sense of territory.

The scenes enacted by the countless insects in our garden don't necessarily have to be colorful in order to enchant. As dusk gathers, the vivacious bridal ballet of puny gnats and mosquitoes is worth our attention. They swirl through the purple twilight of the evening in quivering columns and in undulating festoons, like a grand finale before sunset. However, it is all but a finale. No sooner has darkness set in than the next act begins: the nocturnal dance of the fireflies and moths.

In some cases, though, I prefer to close my eyes and listen. On warm days in June I sit, eyes closed, under the rhododendron, which around that time of the year is a solid canopy of lilac flowers. It is alive with bees and bumblebees. A thousand little busybodies drone about all day long, and if I sit there long enough, it is almost as if their monotonous buzzing vibrates within my head. It ceases to be a thousand different voices, it takes on a quality of magic, and slowly it melts into a single sound, like one prolonged, trembling, soothing note played on an enormous cello.

Please don't speak. Don't shatter this moment of sheer magic. Above all, don't mistake me for a lonely soul who needs cheering up. You are wrong to think that I'm alone, hiding from the evil world. I am very busy being bugged. By bugs.

Wasps!

I REALIZE that my list of bugs in the previous chapter is incomplete, but unfortunately it is not possible to describe the myriad different crawlies that populate my garden. You may wonder why I didn't elaborate on the omnipresent ladybug, who, like a true lady, has many other dresses in her wardrobe besides her familiar black polka-dotted number; did you know that she also comes in unobtrusive beige, or in anything between the very lightest shade of yellow and the deepest orange, or in black, or even checkered, like a chessboard? You may be disappointed at the total absence of some ethereal lacewings and clumsy chafers. You may not agree with the silence that I maintained around some particularly noisy critters: crickets and grasshoppers. I also failed to elaborate on the clownish, clumsy daddy longlegs, who appear around sunset on mild summer evenings and gambol aimlessly along the hedges, and I never even mentioned the peculiarly noisy bluebottles — I prefer to call them bumbleflies — who, though generally despised, resemble flying jewels with their stunning display of steely greens and blues. Believe me, they are all present and they all faithfully attend the critters' garden party, which continues all through the summer. But an enumeration of *all* the bugs in my garden would make these pages look rather like an arthropodal memorial.

To one other group, however, I would like to draw your special attention. I already briefly mentioned them: wasps.

Wasps. The very word is enough to make one shudder. It evokes visions of folded newspapers swatting through the air in attempts to chase away these buzzing pests. Of screaming toddlers fleeing from the picnic table. Of panicking parents trying to protect their very young. The most peaceful gathering is rudely disrupted when the party is joined by one — but usually more — of these uninvited guests. "*A WASP!!*" shouts the oldest daughter, and drops her ice cream cone on the lawn. Mother's motherly smile vanishes instantaneously. "Oh dear, do be careful!" she mumbles, looking a trifle pale. "Nothing to be afraid of! Don't move! Don't panic!" shouts Father, but a wild look in his eyes betrays that he is very close to panic himself. He grabs the Sunday supplement, folds it in half, and a period of hunting ensues . . . Does it sound familiar?

It must be admitted that the wasp's bad reputation is not entirely unfounded. Some of us are allergic to its sting, and if that is the case, one has to exercise extreme caution, of course. Unfortunately, the wasp's status of aggressor is grossly exaggerated, because the truth is that for the most part of its short life cycle, a wasp is no bother to us at all and will never attack us, unless it feels trapped or we come too close to the nest. On the contrary, few other insects are more useful in our ceaseless struggle against aphids, caterpillars, and other destructive bugs. If you keep your eyes open, you might discover this for yourself. I did, quite accidentally, some years ago, and from that moment on I left the ranks of the Wasp Haters Club and became a fervent pro-Vespidaeist.

It all began on a warm evening in May. I was sitting in the garden in a state of blissful idleness, listening to the sounds of the night. Not the sounds of civilization, which I try to ban from my hearing at all costs, but Mother Nature's 1001 little voices that always surround us, particularly the ones that speak to us after dark: the flutter of a moth's wings, the chant of the wind in the trees, the hoarse croak of an insect-hunting toad. To me these sounds are as much a part of the garden as any of my flowers and shrubs. I know them all. And so do you, for not so long ago I invited you to attend a special performance of this nocturnal symphony.

On this particular night my ears caught an unfamiliar sound, much like a mouse chewing a nut. It puzzled me. The sound came from one of the tall conifers, and conifers do not bear nuts. It also came from about twelve feet above me, and to the best of my knowledge well-educated mice don't climb trees, unless there is a reward. Finally, the sound was very weak, too weak for an adult mouse . . .

I don't mind mice. On the contrary, I find them rather endearing, as long as they stay outside. But since I had just been through a nerve-racking experience (of which I told you in a previous chapter; they consumed my curtains, remember?), my MTL — Mouse Tolerance Level — was extremely low, and I didn't appreciate their presence in the garden. So I clapped my hands and I shook the tree, and the perpetrator should have darted off in terror. The sound should have stopped. Only it didn't. The gnawing went on and on and on, and I realized I was dealing with a creature that, however small, knew no fear. But it was too dark to see anything, and even a flashlight could not shed light on the matter.

I continued my investigation first thing in the morning, and this time I was rather more successful. Though the sound had stopped, or had become inaudible on account of numerous horticultural activities in neighboring gardens, I discovered something hanging under one of the branches: a grayish globular object about the size of a tennis ball. There was some activity as well: yellow-and-black striped insects were coming and going through a tiny hole in the bottom. Yellow jackets!!

My first reaction was to dash off to the telephone and summon the village exterminator there and then. But almost immediately two thoughts occurred to me: what had the poor creatures done wrong to justify their total obliteration, and what could they possibly do wrong in the very near future? Until now I had not even noticed their presence; surely there was no reason for alarm. So I rejected the possibility of human intervention and I allowed them to stay, for the time being, at least.

That summer I spent a good deal of time wasp-watching. It was beyond any doubt worth it, and as the weeks went by I realized once more the privilege of being allowed to observe yet another one of nature's miracles, right here in my own garden. I marveled at the indefatigable and ceaseless activities of these insects. Their vespiary, like an exotic fruit strangely out of place on a conifer branch, grew and grew until it attained the size of a small, almost perfectly shaped football. Inside, I knew from newly purchased insect books, life was buzzing on as well. A queen was producing offspring, and hundreds of larvae were fed the livelong day. Their diet met with my full approval: aphids, caterpillars, flies, and slugs fell victim to the stings and jaws of the wasp workers at an incredible rate, and the display of strength and ingenuity when carrying entire bugs back to their nest was quite amazing.

In the meantime most neighbors began to express, in various degrees of frankness, their doubts about my sanity, but I maintained my tolerant attitude toward "my" wasps. And I had my reward: after several weeks I became aware of an unusual absence of garden pests, and the fact that for once I did not have to destroy colonies of caterpillars or cut away aphid-laden digitalis plants I put down to the doings of these black-and-yellow workers. They in turn were rewarded: I left them undisturbed all summer. They lived, after all, at a safe distance of twelve feet up, and rarely did they find their way down to my lemonade or summer pudding. And no, not once was I stung.

Just as my wasp experiment had started at night, it ended at night. One afternoon toward the very end of that summer a light wind arose, and by the time dusk was gathering it had increased to a ferocious gale. All night it whistled and howled around the house, but at dawn it subsided. As soon as I was dressed I went out into the garden to survey the damage. Miraculously, there was none. But the wasps had been less lucky. Not only had their homestead sustained damage (I found a tiny piece of their papery palace between the hydrangeas), it had become nonexistent. Not a single particle of it was left under that familiar branch.

I felt a sudden emptiness. Inevitably I thought back to that day in May when I had first discovered the nest. I had almost called for the exterminator, but in time I had decided against such action. In return I had been rewarded with endless pleasure, as well as a valuable lesson. Now this lesson had ended on a familiar theme: nothing lasts. Once more, I mused, nature had taken the ultimate decision by employing, with perfect timing, her own exterminator.

The Green Millennium

O UR MILLENNIUM is drawing to its close. Indeed, by the time you read these words, you may
have already crossed this bridge to the future,
and the Age of Space Odyssey may well be on its way into
history. The question is, were we prepared for an occasion so rare that it is not even a once-in-a-lifetime affair?
Did we ever realize that only once before in our era did
humanity live to witness the transition of one Christian
millennium into another? Should we celebrate?

If you ask me, I think we should, most definitely, if
it is not too late. We should festoon the entire world
with garlands that will reach from one continent to another and bring the people together. An impractical and

whimsical suggestion, maybe, of which I'm nevertheless very much in favor. Our earth, though in a sorry state, is our most precious possession, so why not deck its entire surface, just this once, and show the universe that we are *all* holding high revel?

Awaiting more detailed guidelines from the Third Millennium Committee (which should be called into existence without further delay), I have meanwhile decided to celebrate its arrival in my own infinitely less spectacular and slightly selfish way: I'll dedicate it to my own garden, and I'll simply declare it the Green Millennium.

Green. A word that I have used countless times throughout these pages. I'm afraid I have been far from unique, for *Green,* it would appear, has been rediscovered all around us during the last decennia of our present millennium. The word is so frequently used that we barely recognize it as a color. It has become a state of mind. It certainly has become my state of mind, and I eagerly follow this trend by using *Green* to indicate matters that are hardly color-related. The song of birds, for instance, is *Green.* The roar of a 747 engine, in contrast, is positively *non-Green.* Silk and cotton are *Green,* as opposed to nylon and dacron, not to forget our double-knit polyester, the favorite material for many a garment, in which generations have merrily slithered through life, developing ugly rashes in the process.

My garden, of course, is *Green* as well as green. So are most of my garden tools, because my need for motorized equipment (*non-Green*) has never been very urgent, the garden being of modest dimensions. On the contrary, I have always opposed their use. Not only because they absorb quantities of costly energy, but also because of their annoying habit of rudely disturbing the peace, on Saturdays and Sundays in particular. If I really want to enjoy the rural silence of a sunny Saturday in my garden, I'm forced to get up at six, which is even earlier than on a regular working day. Only then can I have my tea in peace, read the mostly *non-Green* headlines in the morning paper, or maybe enjoy a chapter or two, with no other sounds in the background than those of the morning birds (*Green!*).

Before long, however, the hubbub of civilization enters the auditory organs. The radiant morning has enticed my neighbor into his garden. I hear the door of his shed creak on its rusty hinges. In vain I hope that today he will limit himself to some harmless raking in his borders. Now, there is a *Green* sound I like: the prongs of a rake scraping through the black earth, smoothing it, airing it. Creating a foundation for new life, so to speak. But of course this is wishful thinking, for within minutes he starts his engine-operated lawnmower, and a very *non-Green* roar immediately overpowers the blackbird's matins. His activity seems contagious. Soon another lawnmower joins in, and another one . . .

I find it impossible to maintain my concentration in this din, and with a sigh I close my book. Never mind; my small lawn needs mowing too, and I bring out my dear old hand-operated machine, which is green in color and *Green* in spirit. It has just been cleaned and sharpened and readjusted, and it glides smoothly through the grass with a happy, soothing, and satisfying *rattle-tattle.* A delicious *Green* fragrance immediately wafts up into the summer morning.

Meanwhile the end of our millennium has visibly spawned its *non-Green* byproducts all around me, and prime among these is the new siding of the house immediately across the lane. It was installed five years ago, but it still looks like new. It has never been painted, is everything-proof, and is obnoxiously white. Though it is obviously meant to look like wood, its shiny appearance remains highly artificial, and no number of years will ever be able to tone it down. It may be convenient for the occupants, but to me it is an eyesore.

Likewise, my left-hand neighbors' new carport, with its appalling corrugated roof, disrupted the color scheme of my border and presented a sorry view. To say nothing of the plastic garden furniture that adorns the concrete patio of the house at the back. Not only is it not *Green,* it is of a nasty orange!

One obvious way to deal with these disturbing elements would have been to shut them out by building a nice brick wall around the house. I did at one time seriously consider this possibility. However, it would be a costly enterprise, and in view of the ominous red numbers on my latest bank statements, it was not expedient. Furthermore, one would almost certainly have needed a special building permit, which in all probability would never be granted. And last but not least, it would look distinctly weird and out of place around my modest cottage. No, a wall, unfortunately, was out of the question, and so was a moat, for my fantasy knows no limits. So I opted for an easier solution: I planted another hedge.

That was five years ago. In retrospect these years flew by, but how well I remember the agony of waiting. That first year nothing happened; the hedge remained a pathetic queue of gloomy green plumes that barely masked the surrounding horrors it was supposed to obscure, including the sarcastic grin of one of my neighbors. It absolutely refused to gain even a fraction of an inch. Winter came and winter went, and one sunny morning in early spring I noticed light green, tiny specks on the tips of the branches: the first promise of new life. One month later these specks had sprouted into baby branches of about half an inch.

Much as I should have delighted in this sudden progress, it depressed me beyond words, for I erroneously calculated that at this rate it would be well into the next millennium before the hedge would even begin to block the surrounding monstrosities from my view. God only knows how many more years before I would be able to hide in the privacy of my own garden, undisturbed by vistas of modern technology. The very thought of having to bridge such an incredible chasm of time was enough to plunge me into the very deepest state of exquisite melancholy.

It is a good thing that I did not convey these splenetic thoughts to my hedge, for it would almost certainly have revenged itself for such blatant lack of confidence. It would have sulked and withered away on the spot. As it was, it not only continued to grow but also accelerated its speed. The gaps between the individual trees began to fill, and halfway through the summer I suddenly discovered that the legs of my neighbor's plastic furniture had become practically invisible. In the course of the year that followed the remainder of their seating arrangement slowly dissolved as well, with only a hint of orange plastic shimmering through the new growth. I could now safely rearrange my own garden furnishings, a collection of dear old wicker chairs with incredible amounts of seating hours and splintering cane sticking into the back of one's thighs and knees. (One of them collapsed one day, the moment one of my guests, a rather obese villager, sat down in it. She tumbled sideways into a flowering rhododendron. Twigs and blossoms snapped, bumblebees buzzed in bewilderment around her, but fortunately she got through this incident unscathed.) Convinced that they could no longer start arguments with their monstrous colleagues from across the way, I placed them in a cozy nook near the hedge, where they continued to live happily ever after, until this very day.

On the other side of the house things began to look up too. My neighbors' car was no longer visible, and of its new housing only the unsightly roof, of a green of unrivaled acidity, still hovered in full view outside my kitchen window. However, the knowledge that it would be a matter of six more solstices at the utmost before this atrocity too would be camouflaged behind lush greenery made it infinitely easier to live with.

Meanwhile the question that literally loomed large on my horizon was, will the house across the road with its repulsive siding be effectively veiled from my panorama? Though it is only a one-story dwelling, it seemed unlikely at the time; a house is a structure with mysterious powers of its own, and it might object to being rendered invisible, if only to annoy me. There was no alternative but to get used to its presence.

I *did* get used to it, of course, for we humans are adaptable and eventually we get used to almost anything.

Therefore I didn't even notice at first how the ever-advancing contaminations of modern life were gradually blocked out. Not until it was time to give my adolescent hedge its first proper trimming, which was last year. True to my principles, I used an old-fashioned pair of garden shears which happily snip-snapped over my hedge. It took me an entire day, and by the time I had completed the task my arms were so painful that I could hardly lift them above shoulder level. Nevertheless, the result was most satisfactory, and as I stood back to admire my work I suddenly realized that a miracle had happened: the house across the road had become almost invisible! Only its low roof peeked out above the hedge. It greeted me, and sort of apologized. "You don't mind me?" it seemed to ask. "After all, though I'm only a roof, I'm one of the essentials of life, and you can't possibly object to me. Look how well I have weathered!" The roof was right, of course; I did not object to it. How could I? Unlike the siding, it had weathered very well indeed, in pleasant shades of green and with intriguing patches of turquoise and orange lichens.

This spring my hedge finally grew into a solid green wall. I had to give it another good clipping, which turned out to be an almost impossible task. To reach the top I had to perform dangerous acrobatic feats on a ladder, and so I made a concession, ostensibly for motives of self-preservation: I bought a monstrous, *non-Green,* electric hedge trimmer, the best and the biggest money could buy. After all, I'm only human, and nothing human is alien to me, and it is sometimes necessary to compromise for comfort's sake. Fortunately, I have to use it only once or twice a year, and I honestly don't believe that this will be too much of a burden to the environment. Neither does it seem too high a price to pay for the assurance that at least my own tiny slice of the Planet Earth will be *Green* in the new millennium.

Beyond the Garden Gate

GARDENING IS NOT strictly a matter of planning and planting, of digging and hoeing, of pruning and sowing. Apart from being all of the above, gardening is, above all, a way of life. For the true gardener, it is possibly the *only* way of life. Without his borders and his beds, his lilies and his lilacs, he would probably pine away and be reduced to a state resembling that of a wilted lettuce on the greengrocer's counter.

Of course, on the face of it, other things always seem more important. There are the very basic occupations, like eating, drinking, and sleeping, or, worse, earning a living, that gobble up a substantial part of our life. But as far as I'm concerned, these are so banal that I only reluctantly mention them. Well, perhaps this is too bold a statement, and not entirely true: a good meal after a day's labor in the garden is a perfect conclusion, and the pleasure of sipping one's favorite drink on a drowsy summer afternoon in the cool green shade of one's own chestnut probably beats even the bliss of spending one's afterlife in paradise. But as to earning a living, I'm not so sure. I can't think of anything more irksome that interferes with the joy of gardening, and I would rather deal with the onslaught of an army of slugs or a devastating gale in late spring. Having to leave the garden for even a single day in order to do something so vulgar as making money makes me feel like a wicked parent leaving a child in the custody of an unqualified nanny.

Unfortunately, I have to be rather more vulgar and wicked than most gardeners, since globetrotting is an essential ingredient of my work. And since at this point you are probably wondering what on earth globetrotting has to do with gardening, let me explain: I'm involved in the interests of a company that owns many large and luxurious vessels. Six months of the year I spend on board these liners, which roam the seven seas and sail far beyond the horizon. In general I rather enjoy adding the world to my working space, and I truly delight in meeting literally thousands of people (I probably shake more hands than the Queen of England), yet each time the garden gate clicks behind me into its catch as I embark on yet another excursion, something in me dies.

Some of you who think of traveling as the greatest possible adventure may now sneer and accuse me of being spoiled. You are probably right; I am blasé, very much so. You will now proclaim in tones of indignation that you would be only too pleased to exchange your pretty little garden for an even prettier *séjour* on some exotic island. That you simply can't wait to set out on an exciting expedition into the very depths of a country so remote that nobody even knows its name. That at any given moment you are more than willing to broaden your horizon by crossing it. But believe me, after 1,972,543 miles of tramping about the world, you may find that countries and regions are no longer exotic, just different. Even the gaudiest orchid will lose some of its luster; instead it will make you long with intense and melancholic yearning for your own simple honeysuckle. The raucous screeches of wild parrots will cease to excite you; they will begin to hurt your eardrums, and you would gladly sacrifice your last crusado or rupee or whatever currency you carry in your wallet for a single minute of the nightingale's song.

Because, you see, you are a true gardener, and you always carry the memory of your own garden in your heart. No matter where on earth you are (or on what other planet, in the unlikely case you should happen to read this in the year 2296), some mysterious tie will always bind you to your very own patch of soil. You can't see a bromeliad without thinking of your mistletoe in the old apple tree. And your first encounter with the gargantuan flower of the *Victoria regia* will make you homesick for your own considerably less majestic water lilies in the modest pond that you dug with your own hands. Only the knowledge that sooner or later — preferably sooner — you will be reunited with all your floral pets, and you will smell the lavender on the south side of the house, and you will see the painted lady butterflies fluttering about the *Sedum spectabile*, will save you from a nervous breakdown. Meanwhile you stroll in sweat-stained cotton prints through the heat and traffic fumes of Rio de Janeiro's flamboyant Copacabana, and you realize how infinitely more pleasant it would be to ramble through the neighboring fields at home, clad in tweeds and twill, with your dog at your heels and an invigorating rain lashing your face.

Please, don't misinterpret me, especially if you live in warmer regions and your back yard happens to be some sort of lush jungle, or even a sliver of golden desert. Any jungle is a miraculous example of nature's botanical architecture, and the healing powers of the desert are not to be underestimated. Nevertheless, your feelings would be the same, albeit the opposite: after the novelty of your first nightingale's concerto wears off, it will get on your nerves. It will keep you awake, and you will find yourself pining for the homely call of the Cockatoo. Or if only that suffocating gray sky would clear up and the sun would penetrate, albeit for one minute, through this bone-chilling dampness. And wouldn't you give a fortune to be able to kick off those heavy boots and frolic barefoot through your own garden and pick an armful of scarlet anthuriums. Because, you see, nowhere but at home are the flowers the most colorful and the scents the sweetest.

Lest you should have reached the conclusion that I suffer from some curious form of xenophobia, I must now hasten to add that on numerous occasions I have enjoyed and envied the beauty of gardens in all corners of the world. I remember a tiny, secluded Athenean courtyard in which an old and gnarled bougainvillea gently embraced fragments of delicately sculptured marble. The luscious sprays of purple mingling with the gold of the Mediterranean sun and a small patch of intense blue, just visible between the rooftops of the old and silent houses, almost moved me to tears. It was a moment of sheer magic. On another occasion I escaped in despair from the picturesque but grubby little harbor on the island of Grenada, where sweaty polyester-clad tourists flocked together in great numbers around countless T-shirt stalls. I rejected the services of 274 tenacious taxi drivers, left the little town of St. George, and walked uphill. Suddenly I found myself all alone in a green and mysterious silence at the derelict botanical gardens. I had entered another world! Here I marveled at an intriguing harmony of hundreds of species of tropical trees and bushes and bromeliad-laden branches and climbers which had been left to fend for themselves but nevertheless thrived, in the true West Indian spirit of laissez faire.

But always there looms in the background the ghost of my own garden. It follows me wherever I go. It immediately links the bright orange of some nameless tropical flower to the blazing oranges and reds of my own familiar berberis in its autumnal finery. The sight of a towering mango tree never fails to leave me wallowing in gloom, as it reminds me of my modest, five-foot-high apple tree with its three apples last year, and probably none this year because of that late frost in spring.

But somehow the magic moment always arrives, and once again I hear the click of my gate, but this time I'm inside. I take a deep breath and look around: oh yes, I had forgotten, it's winter. The trees are bare. The perennials are asleep (I swear I can hear them snore), and the annuals are gone. It is almost like a dream: only twelve hours ago I stood face to branch with an unfamiliar tropical tree; so dazzling was its heavy load of scarlet flowers that it made me swoon with delight, and still its image lingers on my retina. Now the only red that welcomes me is that of a single lonely rose, caught and preserved by the first spell of frost. A more striking contrast in such a short span of time is hardly conceivable. Yet nothing in the world could induce me to exchange this rose for an entire wood of tropical trees, however magnificent. Because for the hundredth time I reach the conclusion that flowers are the most fragrant, fruits are the sweetest, and, in spite of a well-known phrase, grass is the greenest on my own side of the garden gate.